FIRST STEPS

IN

ENGLISH LITERATURE.

BY

ARTHUR GILMAN, A.M.,

AUTHOR OF "FIRST STEPS IN GENERAL HISTORY," "SEVEN HISTORIC AGES," ETC.

"The love of letters is friendly to sober manners and virtuous conduct, which in every profession is the road to success and to respect."—Henry Mackenzie, in "The Lounger.

A. S. BARNES & COMPANY

NEW YORK, CHICAGO, NEW ORLEANS.

BY THE SAME AUTHOR.

FIRST STEPS IN GENERAL HISTORY. A Suggestive Outline. 1 vol., 16mo, with Maps and Charts. Pp. 400.

"We have been delighted with the simplicity of the plan and the care with which it has been executed. . . . . The number of facts which the author has compressed into these outline sketches is really surprising; the chapters on the Middle Ages and Feudalism afford striking examples of his power of succinct but comprehensive statement. In his choice of representative periods and events in the histories of Nations he shows very sound judgment, and his characterization of conspicuous historical figures is accurate and impartial." — *Literary World.*

SEVEN HISTORIC AGES; or, Talks about Kings, Queens, and Barbarians. 1 vol., 16mo, with illustrations.

"Mr. Gilman is a scholar who knows how to write historical sketches for the young with accuracy, vivacity, and attractiveness." — *Intelligencer.*

"The work is excellently done, and the book will be read by children with real pleasure." — *Literary World.*

"There is an airy grace about the little book that leaves a charming impression." — MRS. HORACE MANN.

PREFACE TO THE TENTH EDITION.

IN treating of the Art of Memory, Francis Bacon tells the student that when an investigation is begun without a "prenotion" of the scope of the subject, "the mind strives and exerts itself, endeavors and casts about in an endless manner." A modern thinker, following out this suggestion, remarks: "Without such an antecedent general apprehension, the mind is at a loss where to begin, and which way to proceed. The true idea of any object is a species of preparatory knowledge which throws light over the whole field of inquiry, and introduces an orderly method into the whole course of examination. It is the clue which leads through the labyrinth."

It was with a desire to furnish the student of the History of English Literature with this "prenotion," this "preparatory knowledge," that the writer prepared the volume now in the reader's hands. He wished to make a useful book, rather than to display his own acquaintance with the subject or his peculiar notions regarding it. His intercourse with schools and teachers led him to sympathize with the sentiment since expressed very forcibly by the president of one of our colleges, that the age demands small text-books,[1] and he therefore determined to omit from his work all that could possibly be spared, and yet leave it a sufficient guide to the learner.

In laying out his work the author first discussed the general divisions of the subject, and found that but two needed to be indicated. These, in turn, fell naturally into four subdivisions each, and thus he had a plan of the simplest description, without resorting to any questionable system of nomenclature, or attempting to mark out divisions where none actually exist. In casting about for names for the divisions thus indicated, the author found the work already done, and it was only necessary for him to adopt those that had stood the test of use, and were supported by the suffrages of scholars who were acknowledged masters of the subject.

Before this book was published there was no concise manual adapted to the use of beginners in the History of English Literature, and the cordiality with which the successive editions have

1 "Small text-books, containing only the essentials of the subjects treated of, only those parts that have life in them, that cannot be eliminated without leaving the subject imperfect, are rare. It takes a brave man, and one merciless towards himself, to make a small, simple, but thorough text-book. Such books we must have, if we use text-books at all." — PRESIDENT CHADBOURNE, of Williams College.

been received prove that it was needed in the schools.

Subsequent study, and an examination of the important works that have been produced in England and America during the past five years, have confirmed the author in the views expressed in this volume. The tenth edition is, therefore, sent forth with much greater satisfaction and confidence than the first was. The public and private expressions of approval with which the book has been favored lead to the belief that in many instances it has accomplished its object by stimulating a love of studies in our beloved literature.

Designing to encourage the student to examine books as entireties, the author has not introduced selections from the writers treated in this manual. Extracts have their appropriate place, but it is the object of this book to send the reader to the library where he is to use the "prenotion" here acquired. Even if the accessible library comprise but few standard authors, it may give aid to the student, who ought to bear in mind the truth, that it is better to have a thorough acquaintance with one writer's works, than a superficial knowledge of the writings of many authors.

A small text-book, such as President Chadbourne commends, cannot be well used by an incompetent instructor. The teacher or lecturer who puts it into his pupils' hands must be prepared to enlarge upon its principles, and to help the learner in carrying forward investigations growing out of it. When the teacher of English Literature does this, he makes his recitations eminently profitable and deeply interesting. Taking up the historical clue given in the manual, the teacher and pupil may together develop more fully than a text-book can the working of the influences there only indicated. Or, again, by making the works of any given author the basis of a critical theme, the same idea may be made operative in a different direction.

Thus a single suggestion of the text-book amplified by the intelligent pupil, under the direction of the experienced teacher, becomes a means of exciting discussion, of giving life to the recitations, of stimulating thought in a most agreeable way, and of begetting enthusiasm for a study that is second to few in importance in a symmetrical educational system.

Let us then enter upon our pursuit with love, putting our hearts into the work, remembering that our unrivaled literature is a noble inheritance from the fathers which we cannot too greatly honor, or too carefully cultivate!

CAMBRIDGE, MASS., *March* 1, 1876.

TABLE OF CONTENTS.

ENGLISH LITERATURE.

CHAPTER I.

HISTORICAL.

IN order to understand the English Language and Literature thoroughly, we need a certain familiarity with the geography and history of England, and other parts of Europe.

We see, by reference to the map, that England is a division of the British Isles, which lie off the western coast of the continent of Europe, only separated from it by a narrow channel. The further back we carry our investigation into its history, the slower and more difficult our progress becomes. One reason of this is, that the language has changed so much that it is as difficult to read as French or Latin, or any other foreign tongue. A second reason is, that very many of the early records are lost.

We know, however, that two thousand years ago Great Britain was inhabited by a rude race called Celts. These were descendants of savage tribes that had come into Europe from Asia at so early a period that history gives us no account of the migration.[1]

Four hundred years before Christ, a branch of this people came in conflict with the powerful Roman nation, and, after considerable hard fighting, sacked the city of Rome. Two hundred and fifty years later another branch attacked the northwestern frontier of the same empire, and was so thoroughly defeated as never again to be heard of as a conquering people.

Fifty-five years before Christ, Julius Cæsar crossed from Gaul into Britain, and, after some battles, received the allegiance of the tribes in the southern part of the island. For three hundred and fifty years the Romans nominally ruled Britain, but their hold upon the government was neither strong nor without interruptions.[2]

About four hundred years after Christ, the Goths under Alaric, aided by the Vandals, attacked and overthrew the city of Rome, and thus compelled the withdrawal of all Roman forces from Britain. The establishment of Christianity was retarded, and the people relapsed into barbarism.

Not long after the departure of the Romans, the Saxon element was introduced. Warriors from parts of Europe now included in German territory invaded the island, and, after a struggle, overcame the natives, and established what is known as the Saxon Heptarchy. This period is full of romance.

[1] Freeman's *Old English History*, ch. i. [2] *Ibid.* ch. ii.

The stories of King Arthur and his knights of the Round Table belong to it, and it is strongly sus pected that Hengist and Horsa, who are said to have led the Saxon invaders, were mythical creations of some unknown bard.

In the year 827, one of the kings of the Heptarchy, Egbert of Wessex, obtained control of all the kingdoms, and, uniting them under one government, called it *Engleland* or England, and himself *Rex gentis Anglorum*, or king of the English people.

Matters continued in this state until 1013, when the Danes, after having made many vain efforts, put the English king to flight, and obtained control of the government. They held the power twenty-eight years. In the year 1041, however, the Saxons again obtained control of the government, and held it for twenty-five years.

In 1066 the Normans came over from Normandy, just across the channel, under the lead of Duke William, now called the *Conqueror*. They met the Saxons under King Harold at Senlac, near Hastings, which is in Sussex, about seventy miles southeast of London. The night before the battle the Normans prayed in silence, and the Saxons sat about their blazing camp-fires eating and drinking, and singing the merry songs of their fathers. In the battle of the next day the Saxons were dispersed, and though fifteen thousand Normans were killed, Duke William had conquered, and became the first of a line of Norman monarchs. Since this time the government of England has never been overthrown by foreign foes.

The Normans ruled from 1066 to 1154, and then Henry II., surnamed Plantagenet, the most powerful monarch of the time, ascended the throne. There were fourteen kings in this celebrated line, of whom the last was Richard III., who was killed at the battle of Bosworth Field, in 1485. Among these was Edward III., who began to reign in 1327, subdued Scotland, invaded France, and in connection with his son, the *Black Prince*, fought the famous battle of Cressy in 1346. The Black Prince died before his father, leaving a son, who, in 1377, became King Richard II. During his reign our great poet Chaucer flourished, and John Wiclif, the herald of the Reformation, died.

After him came Henry IV., of the house of Lancaster, whose reign was full of disturbances. He was succeeded by Henry V., who conquered France, after the battles of Harfleur and Agincourt. The next reign was very stormy. The French wars continued, and the *Maid of Orleans* led the French army from victory to victory, and though she was captured and inhumanly burned to death by the English, her countrymen regained their territory. Insurrections and conspiracies were rife in Britain, and at the end of Henry VI.'s reign the crown passed to the house of York in the person of Edward IV. During his reign the first printing-press was set up in England, by William Caxton.

Richard III. closed the line of Plantagenets, and the strife between the houses of York and Lancaster, called the *Wars of the Roses*, which for forty years had distracted the kingdom, ceased. Many colleges and schools were founded at this period, books were a little more extensively circulated, and the language became more refined and uniform.

The house of Plantagenet, and the houses of Lancaster and York, were succeeded by the house of Tudor, which gave England five of her most illustrious sovereigns. Henry VII. was the first, and Queen Elizabeth was the last of this line. The period of the rule of the house of Tudor includes the time of the discovery of America by Columbus in 1492, many religious disturbances, and the lives of some of the most remarkable authors of whom we shall have to speak.

James I., son of Mary Queen of Scots, became king at the death of Elizabeth. He began the Stuart dynasty in England, being descended, as was claimed, from a son of Banquo, who was murdered by Macbeth in the eleventh century. To this family belonged, also, Charles I. and II., and James II., the last of whom was dethroned in 1689. The rule of the Stuarts was interrupted by what is called the period of the *Commonwealth*. This extended from 1649 to 1660, during which time the Puritans, or Roundheads, under Oliver Cromwell obtained ascendency over the Royalists, or Cavaliers, under Charles I., and having beheaded that king, governed the country with great strictness, until the restoration of the royal family in the person of Charles II. During the reign of the Stuarts the settlements at Jamestown in Virginia, and at Plymouth in Massachusetts, were made in America.

The reign of James II. was marked by so many horrors, owing specially to the ferocious deeds of Judge Jeffreys, that it has been called the Reign of Terror. It ended with the dethronement of the king, and the establishment of the joint house of Stuart and Nassau.

Mary, daughter of James II., had married William, Prince of Orange, and in 1689 this couple was called to the throne. During their reign, which was marked by war and treachery, the present heavy national debt of England was begun. In 1702 William died, and the sceptre fell to Anne, a sister of his wife. During her reign the brilliant campaigns of the Duke of Marlborough occurred, England and Scotland were permanently united, and so many superior literary productions appeared that Oliver Goldsmith called it the *Augustan Age* of English literature.

In 1714 the present house of Brunswick began to reign in the person of George I., who was a great grandson of James I. He was followed by George II. and III., who both had stormy reigns. During the latter the war of the American Revolution occurred, and subsequently the War of 1812, for

George III. ruled sixty years. During tne same period, also, Napoleon Bonaparte revolutionized the politics of Europe.

George IV. reigned from 1820 to 1830, and was followed by his brother, William IV., who died in 1837, when Victoria I., a granddaughter of George III., ascended the throne at the age of eighteen, and England was at peace with all the world.

CHAPTER II.

DEFINITION OF TERMS.

NGLAND was known to the Romans as Britannia, and also as Anglia. The latter name is said to have been derived from Angeln in Schleswig. Angeln is a little tract of country laid down on the map of Denmark. It is bounded on the east by the Baltic Sea, on the north by Flensburg Bay, and on the south by the river Schley. It is not known when the first emigrants from the land of the Teutons came into Britain, nor is it supposed that they all came from Angeln. A number of different tribes were undoubtedly involved in the movement, but the Angles took a greater part of the land than any of the others, and therefore the whole country received their name in the end.

The Celts lived in Britain and on the continent, at the earliest known period. Julius Cæsar called them *Gauls* in one branch, and *Belgians* in another. They were also called Cimbrians. The *Gael* of Scotland, Ireland, and Wales represent other branches of the Celts.

Anglo-Saxon is a modern term used to designate

in a general way all the Teutonic settlers in Britain. The Teutonic race, which originated in Asia, is divided into three branches.

I. The first branch is mainly composed of the *Teutonic* inhabitants of upper and middle Germany, Switzerland, and Hungary.

II. The second is called the *Saxon* branch, and includes the Frisians, Old Saxons, or Low Germans, the Dutch, Flemings, and Saxons of Transylvania, the English, Scotch, and most of the inhabitants of the United States.

III. The third is the *Scandinavian* branch, and includes the Swedes, Norwegians, Icelanders, and Danes.

The word *Teuton* is only another form of our word Dutch, and has always been applied to those we call Germans. It is derived from *Tuisco*, a god or hero whom that people considered their common ancestor.

The Jutes are a wide-spread branch of the Teutonic race which inhabited the irregular peninsula of Jutland, bounded by the North Sea, the Skager-Rack, and the Baltic. The present kingdom of Denmark covers nearly the same territory.

Frisia is the ancient name of the most northerly division of Holland, now called Friesland. The name was also applied to a portion of Hanover about Aurich.

Literature is — excluding the recorded knowledge of the positive sciences — the entire result of knowledge and fancy preserved in writing. Literature proper is addressed to man as man, and is catholic, universal, not exclusive. It is adapted to strengthen rather than to store the mind. A treatise on arithmetic or geometry is, therefore, not a part of literature proper, for it does not appeal to its readers as men, but as students in the pursuit of knowledge of a special kind. The works of Shakespeare, on the other hand, do belong to literature, because they appeal to us all as human beings, and not to any class of men in particular. Literature is found in many different languages. This book treats only of that found in the English language.

Linguistics is the science that treats of languages, and a person skilled in languages is called a *linguist.*

Philology is the study of the words of a language. It is a term used by different authors in different significations. It was originally applied in Germany to the study of the languages of Greece and Rome, as a means of general culture. Dr. Samuel Johnson defined it *criticism, grammatical learning,* in which sense it includes, —

I. *Etymology,* or the science of the origin of words;

II. *Grammar,* or the science of the construction of language or languages; and

III. That part of *Literary Criticism* which investigates the merits or demerits of style or diction, as compared with a received standard.

Comparative Philology, more properly called the *Science of Language*, is the science which treats of the laws and properties of all languages.

We find that English Literature takes either the form of *Prose* or *Verse*, each of which general divisions is subdivided into other classes.

Poets are those writers who so combine the materials of the natural and moral world, as to present them in new shapes, or in unaccustomed or affecting points of view, and in metrical language.

Prose Writers are those who produce composition not in verse, and without metre, or poetic measure.

Verse is at a very early period in the history of our literature found in the form of

Lyrics, so called, because among the ancients they were sung to the lyre. The name is now applied to poetry suitable for music, which is generally the earnest expression of the composer's thoughts and feelings. In this class are, —

1. *Ballads*, which are either sentimental songs, light poems, or lyric tales in verse.

2. *Pastorals*, or poems descriptive of shepherds or their occupations, or of country life. *Idyls* are properly pastorals, though the name is frequently given to highly wrought descriptive poems on other subjects.

3. *Odes*, or short lyrics that express sentiment, but do not generally admit of narrative.

4. *Hymns,* or lyrics intended for singing in religious service, though they are not always adapted to music. It is said that a complete hymn should consist of a central creative thought shaping itself into melodious utterance, with every detail subordinated to its clear and harmonious presentation.

5. *Elegies,* or poetical compositions of a mournful character.

Epics are considered the highest style of poetry. They relate the history of real or imaginary events of elevated character. Where the theme is not an action but a hero, it is called a *Heroic poem.* Among the world's epics are Homer's *Iliad,* Virgil's *Æneid,* Dante's *Divina Commedia,* and Milton's *Paradise Lost.*

Dramatic Poetry is that in which the action or narrative is not related, but represented. It is found in the form of *Tragedy,* in which the human passions and the woes and misfortunes of life are represented in such a manner as to excite grief, pity, indignation, or horror; and of *Comedy,* in which the lighter faults, passions, and follies of mankind are represented.

The productions of Prose writers may be considered in four principal divisions.

I. *History,* or the narration of past events. Philosophical or universal history is that which seeks the laws of human events, the principle which develops nations and civilizations, and the forces which move the world onward to its destiny. Bunsen says it is "that most sacred epic or dramatic poem, of which God is the poet, humanity the hero, and the historian the prophetical interpreter." Under this head we must consider —

1. *Annals*, in which past events are digested in series according to years.

2. *Biography*, or the history of the life of individuals.

3. *Travel*, or the history of occurrences or observations in a journey or travel.

II. *Fiction*, under which we may include all literature of the imagination and fancy. It includes —

1. *The Novel*, which is longer than a fable, presents a plot and a number of characters, and generally treats of occurrences and manners of recent times.

2. *The Romance*, which treats of wild adventure, generally of a remote period, especially of the age of chivalry, and usually connected with love or war. Romances are so called because first written in the Romance languages. The earliest were founded upon the lives and deeds of King Arthur and the Emperor Charlemagne.

3. *Dramatic Prose*, which is of the same nature as dramatic verse.

III. *Oratory*, as a division of literature, includes compositions of an argumentative or persuasive character usually intended for oral delivery. It includes —

1. *Sacred Oratory*, or that which treats of rhetorical compositions intended for delivery from the pulpit.

2. *Forensic Oratory*, treating of those delivered in courts of law.

3. *Deliberative Oratory*, treating of those pronounced in deliberative bodies.

IV. *Scientific Prose* is that which relates to knowledge methodically digested or arranged. We may consider it under three divisions.

1. *Theology*, which includes all that relates to the existence, nature, and attributes of God, and of his relations to man.

2. *Metaphysics*, which treats of the philosophy of the mind.

3. *Physics*, which treats of all things which exist independent of the mind's conception of them.

THIS TABLE EXHIBITS THE PRINCIPAL BRANCHES OF THE ARYAN OR INDO-EUROPEAN LANGUAGES.

THE ARYAN SPEECH.

Indic.	*Iranic.*	*Hellenic.*	*Celtic.*	*Romanic.*	*Slavonic.*	*Gothic.*
Or Language of India.	Used in Persia, Armenia, etc.	Including Doric, Attic, and Modern Greek.	Found in Wales, Brittany, Scotland, and the Isle of Man.	Used in Italy, Spain, France, and Portugal.	Used in Russia, Poland, Bohemia, and Lithuania.	Found in Germany, Holland, Friesland, Denmark, Sweden, Iceland, Norway and England.

⁂ The languages of Finland, Lapland, and Hungary, belong to the *Uralic* division, named from the mountains of that name. This is a branch of the great class called by Max Müller *Turanian*. F. W. Farrar, an excellent authority, calls this class *Sporadic*, with reference to the fact that the languages are more scattered than those of the two other classes; or *Allophylian*, with reference to their being spoken by other different tribes from those belonging to the *Aryan* and *Semitic* races.

CHAPTER III.

LANGUAGES OF EUROPE. — PERIODS OF ENGLISH LITERATURE.

THE principal languages of Europe may be divided into five classes.

I. The *Celtic*, now found only in the Highlands of Scotland, the wildest parts of Ireland, the Isle of Man, the mountainous regions of Wales and in Brittany (Armorica). The Celts led in the early emigration from the East, and their language, after having crossed over the whole European continent, is now only found lingering on its extreme western borders, where it is year by year losing its claim to be considered a living speech.

II. The *Romanic*, which is found in Italy, France, Spain, and Portugal. The languages of these countries are so called, because they originated in that of the ancient Romans, and they exhibit evident traces of their Latin origin.

III. The *Gothic*, called also Germanic, or Teutonic. This class includes the languages of Norway, Sweden, Denmark, and Iceland, which are called Norse, or Scandinavian; the English; the Frisic, only found in the Netherlands, and which is not used in books; the Flemish and Dutch; and the German proper.

IV. The *Slavonic*, of which the principal divisions are the Russian and Polish. This class covers a vast extent of country in Europe, Asia, and North America.

V. The *Uralic*, used by the Finns, Hungarians, and Laplanders. It receives its name from the Ural Mountains, and extends into Asia.

A glance at the map of Europe will show that the migrations of the nations have pushed the *Celtic* languages to the extreme western verge of that continent; that the *Romanic* are confined to the southern part; the *Slavonic* to the eastern; and the *Uralic* to the northern countries; while the great central portion is occupied by nations speaking the *Gothic* tongues. This distribution of languages is not an arrangement of man, but the fulfillment of a design which has governed the movements of nations for many generations.

Turning now to the branch of the Gothic language which we use, we find that its literature, which is the expression of the national mind, has at different periods considerably varied in its form. This does not imply any change in its character, for that was thoroughly English in its underlying nature all the while.

Let us now inquire what these changes of form are, and what influences have been exerted upon the English mind to cause them.

These queries are partially answered in subsequent chapters, but to discuss them thoroughly would demand a careful study of English history, and an examination of the history, literature, and geographical relations of the neighboring countries. It would demand also an inquiry into the manners, morals, and customs of them all.

Our Literature lies before us in two great periods.

I. *Immature English*, beginning with an indefinite date in the remote past, and ending about the middle of the sixteenth century. It may be said to end with the accession of Queen Elizabeth, in the year 1558.

II. *Mature English*, or the period from the year 1558 to the present time.

Any classification of the history of our language and literature into periods is subject to adverse criticism; for it is not true that at any defined date one form of style or expression was dropped and another assumed; but it is sufficient to say, with regard to the above division, that while the schoolboy of to-day is able to read with ease and pleasure all that has been written since the days of Elizabeth, most of what comes to us from an earlier date is only understood with the help of a glossary, or after special study. The language of the writers since 1558 is substantially our own, and is properly called modern, though as will be shown it has passed through various stages of growth. So also, previous to the reign of Elizabeth the immature English experienced changes. These latter will be understood if we consider that period in four divisions.

I. *Original English*, ending with the year 1150. This is sometimes spoken of as the Saxon or Anglo-Saxon period, as if one language then used had been subsequently changed for another; but, as has been shown by the highest authorities, the changes have been very gradual, and as our tongue has always been called English, it is better for us to use the above name. The period is sometimes called that of *Stability*, as the language remained in material points unchanged.

II. *Broken English*, from 1150 to 1250, during which period contact with languages of different origin, broke up the original form of the English. It is sometimes called the *Semi-Saxon*, *Very Early English*, or period of *Disintegration.*

III. *Dead English*, from 1250 to 1350. During this century there was very little change in the language. The Latin was used in our literature, and the vernacular, though still the speech of the people, was disparaged and little used in literature. No distinct tendency was visible, and it has been called the period of *Stagnation*, or simply of *Old English.*

IV. *Reviving English*, extends from 1350 to 1558, and is sometimes called the period of *Resurrection*, or *Middle English.* During all this time the language was receiving rich materials from various sources, and was becoming so free and flowing, so harmonious and forcible as to be fit to convey the noble conceptions of Shakespeare and Milton to our minds and hearts. This was the era of Chaucer, who encouraged his countrymen to leave Latin to the learned, French to the French, and to show their own fancies in the speech of their mothers. Under such influences the language entered upon a new existence, was the speech of all England, and was honored.

We have now reached the end of the period of Immaturity. We have said that since 1558 the language and literature have been subjected to influences that have left permanent marks upon them. These differ from those we have just considered in that they affect the literature more than they do the language.

Four principal influences have been manifest in English Literature during its period of maturity.

I. *The Italian Influence*, extending from the accession of Queen Elizabeth in 1558, to the execution of Charles I., in 1649. Leo X. had been Pope, and the great Italian patron of letters, and the influence of the learned men whom he encouraged was exerted upon all the literatures of Europe. We shall see that it modified that of our language.

II. *The Puritan Influence*, nominally covering only the eleven years between 1649 and 1660, during which the Puritans were in the ascendant. It really was exerted, however, both before and after that period, and writers who sympathized with the Puritans to a greater or lesser extent produced works that are still admired, and some which have not since been excelled.

III. *The French Influence* is apparent from 1660 to 1700. It was occasioned by the overthrow of the Puritan rule and the return of Charles II. from France, where he had resided in the luxurious and gay court of Louis XIV., for a number of years.

IV. *The People's Influence* may be said to have begun with the year 1700, and to have continued to the present time. It was inaugurated by Daniel De Foe, the author of *Robinson Crusoe*, and the founder of the English novel. During this period the popular taste has varied considerably, and four subdivisions will render these variations more clear.

A. *The Age of Pope*, from 1700 to 1745, may be said to have been marked by efforts after elegance and polish, as the highest qualities of good style.

B. *The Age of Johnson*, from 1745 to 1800, was characterized by a predominance of the strength, depth, and earnestness which the eminence of Johnson caused others to imitate.

C. *The Age of Poetical Romance*, from 1800 to 1830. A remarkable number of poets crowd the annals of this period. German influence is apparent, and the writings of the period are marked by taste, emotion, and romance.

D. *The Age of Prose Romance*, in which we notice the culmination of the people's influence, dates from the accession of William IV. in 1830, and still continues. Sir Walter Scott's influence through his *Waverley Novels*, more than that of any other single author, caused the ascendency of prose over poetry. Notwithstanding that prose romance has been more to the popular taste than other styles of composition, it has not been the only kind cultivated, and as we consider the vast and erudite works of Macaulay, Carlyle, Froude, Prescott, Motley, and others, the suspicion is forced upon us that we are approaching an era when historical writings shall predominate.

CHAPTER IV.

PERIOD OF IMMATURITY.

Original English. Previous to 1150.

HAVING in the previous chapters defined the terms necessary to be used, and having shown the divisions under which our subject may be viewed, we shall now proceed to consider each period somewhat more in detail, with some reference to the writers we find in them.

We have observed that this, the earliest stage of the history of our language, is sometimes called the Anglo-Saxon period, but as the writers of the time never so called it, we use the term English, and treat the language as our own tongue, though in its cradle, which in reality it was.

"Not a single drop of foreign blood," says Max Müller,[1] "has entered into the organic system of the English language. The grammar, the blood, the soul of the language, is as pure and unmixed in English as spoken in the British Isles, as it was when spoken on the German Ocean by the Angles, Saxons, and Jutes of the continent." Others might be cited to the same effect; but, after hearing so

[1] Vol. i. p. 81. Scribner's Edition.

IMMATURE ENGLISH.

This chart exhibits the progress of English Literature,— its Periods — the authors mentioned in Gilman's* First Steps, *— and hints at the Contemporary History.

A. D. 600 | 700 | 800 | 900 | 1000 | 1100 | 1200 | 1300 | 1400 | 1500

Romans from B. C. 55–A. D. 449.
Saxons, 449–827.
Anglo-Saxons, 827–1013.
Danes, 1013–1041.
Saxons, 1041–1066.
Normans, 1066–1154.
Wm. Conqueror, 1087.
Wm. II., 1100.
Henry I., 1135.
Stephen, 1154.
Plantagenet.
Henry II., 1189
Richard I., 1199.
John, 1216.
Henry III., 1272.
Edward I., 1307.
Edward II., 1327.
Edward III., 1377.
Richard II., 1399.
Lancaster and York.
Henry IV., 1413.
Henry V., 1422.
Henry VI., 1471.
Edward IV., 1483.
Edward V., 1483.
Richard III., 1485.

Original English. A. D. 1150.	Broken.	Dead.	1350. Reviving. 1558.
Beowulf. Cædmon. King Alfred. Alfric. National Chronicle.	Layamon. Ormulum. Ancren Riwle.	Roger Bacon. Rob't Grosseteste. Robert Mannyng.	Mandeville. John Wiclif. Piers Plowman. Geoffrey Chaucer. John Gower. Bishop Pecocke. Thomas Malory. Sir Thomas More. John Skelton. Bishop Latimer. Archbishop Cranmer. Sir John Cheke. Nicholas Udall. Roger Ascham. Miles Coverdale. John Knox.

Charlemagne, 742–814
Egbert, d. 839?
Alfred the Great, d. 901.
Cambridge University founded, 644?
Oxford University founded, 872?

787. First Danish Invasion.
937. Battle of Brunanburh.
980. Another Danish Invasion.

Edward the Confessor, d. 1066.
Canute the Great, 995–1035.
1st Crusade, 1096–99.
2d Crusade, 1149.
3d Crusade, 1192.
4th Crusade, 1204.
Children's Crusade, 1213.
Magna Charta, 1215.
5th Crusade, 1228.
Richard, Lion Heart, 1157–1199.

Papal power at its greatest height, 1073–1090.
Battles.
Cressy, 1346.
Bannockburn, 1314.
Poictiers, 1356.
Agincourt, 1415.
Printing invented 1440.

Joan of Arc, 1412–1431.
Copernicus, 1473–1543.
Michael Angelo, 1474–1563.
Lorenzo de Medici, 1492

high an authority, it does not appear to be necessary.

The English mind was active at a very early period, but the fruits of its study were for ages recorded to a great extent in the Latin language, because that was considered permanent. Latin was also the channel of the learning of early times, the language of the Church, and readers on the continent, who were the principal readers of the day, were unacquainted with English. Much, therefore, that tended to form the English language, literature, and character was expressed in Latin.

This circumstance retarded the development of our literature, and it did not reach its highest stage in this period until the reign of Alfred the Great, who was born in 841 and died in 901.

In all literatures the first expression is found in rude poetry, because song is the speech of feeling, and emotion seeks utterance before men are educated to the exercise of logic in reasoning. Hence, in the pagan days of England, as in early periods in other countries, we find a class of persons called Gleemen or Bards, whose business it was to recite or sing their poems. The history of the British bard is interesting, because from the labors of those in his humble calling much has arisen to influence the nation. The *trouveurs* or *troubadours* of France, the *scalds* of the Scandinavians, and the *rhapsodists* of the Greeks, belonged to the same general class. The *minnesingers* of Germany, who did not arise until several hundred years later, are not to be confounded with the bards, for they differed from them in important particulars.

A late writer gives us a view of one of these early publishers of literature. "We enter," he says, "one of the great festive halls to join in the ale-drinking, and hear the gleeman's song. The hall is long and wide, say two hundred feet by forty, with a high roof and curved gables. There is at each extremity an entrance in the middle of the wall protected by a porch, that is continued at its farther end to form cellar and pantry. We pass into the hall, a spacious nave with narrow side-aisles. Pillars, dividing aisles from nave, support the central roof. The nave is the great hall itself, and down the middle of its floor run the stone hearths, upon which blaze great timber fires. At the upper end is the raised seat of the chief at a cross-bench, where his wife, who fills the cups of the guests, and his familiar thanes (noblemen), or those whom he distinguishes, sit near him. On each side of the long hearth there runs a line of tables, at which sit the people who are the chief's 'hearth-sharers.' At the lower end, at the space corresponding with the dais, is a table for the drinking-cups. Between the rows of pillars and the outer walls, spaces are parted off within the narrow aisles for sleeping-benches of the warriors. In some of the spaces are the gilded vats of liquor into which the pails of the cup-bearers are dipped.

If women sleep in the hall, the recesses of the pillars behind the dais are kept sacred to them, and there are in the aisles, if the hall be the chief's dwelling, distinct enclosures for the occupation of the family. The sleeping space behind the pillars might perhaps be parted from the hall by paneling and tapestry. In such a hall the gleeman often chanted to his harp, now one adventure, now another, as the guests or their lord might call for this or that favorite incident." [1]

In such a hall as is thus described, we are to picture to ourselves the baron and his retainers calling upon the rough man of letters to enliven the dull moments of the feast with portions of our earliest English poem, the long collection of alliterative lines that contains the romantic tale of *Beowulf*.

The only manuscript of the Beowulf is now preserved in the British Museum, and has been the cause of much learned discussion. This copy was apparently made about the time of the Norman Conquest. It is of British origin, and the original must have been produced as far back as the seventh or eighth century. The poem is heroic, of more than six thousand lines, and, though not reliable as a source of historical information, is very valuable as giving a vivid glimpse of life and customs at the period. It is full of naïve and quaint conceits, and of expressive compound words. Among the latter are the following: *War-fierce*, *mead-house*, *folk-*

[1] Morley's *English Writers*, vol. i. p. 252

stead, winter's-tide, shore-cliffs, wave-paths, weapon-bearers, far-dwellers, home-defenders, glee-wood, hand-gripe, sword-wielders.

Leaving the tale of Beowulf, which is but one of a class of ancient poems of disputed origin, we find the name of *Cædmon,* on the list of poets in the age of Original English. Little is known of the personal history of this author. He was a monk, and his home was in the monastery of Whitby, at the mouth of the river Eske, in the present county of York. His poem is of great value in itself, and of even greater value as one of the influences exerted upon the mind of John Milton. We first hear of it in an account written by another monk, celebrated as the Venerable Bede, who wrote a few years later. It was first published in 1655, only twelve years before the publication of Milton's *Paradise Lost.* Like Milton, this early poet begins with the fall of the rebel angels, sings of the creation of light, of Satan and his host, and their place of torment, their consultations, of Adam and Eve, paradise, the fall, etc., and continues to paraphrase much of the subsequent history of our race, as recorded in the Bible. He begins thus: —

"For us it is very right that we praise with our words, love in minds, the Keeper of the Heavens, Glory-King of Hosts. He is the source of power, the head of all His great creation, Lord Almighty. He never had beginning nor was made, nor cometh any end to the Eternal Lord; but His power is everlasting over heavenly thrones. With high majesty, faithful and strong, He ruleth the depths of the firmament that were set wide and far for the children of glory, the guardians of souls."

KING ALFRED, 841–901. In the person of Alfred the Great we have an author of merit, who possessed at an early age a love for his country, and a strong attachment to its old national poetry. He learned the Latin language late in life, for the purpose of translating writings from it into his vernacular; and beside his own labors he caused learned men, whom he employed, to do the same. By these means he provided for the people a number of books in their own speech. Among his works, the most important is the translation of *Bede's Ecclesiastical History*. At the time of his death he was engaged upon a version of the Psalms.

ALFRIC, ——–1006, Archbishop of Canterbury, called the Grammarian, from a *Latin Grammar* that he translated, was a considerable contributor to the literature of the period. He wrote eighty *Homilies* in the language of the common people, which are simple expositions of doctrines.

THE SAXON CHRONICLE,——–1154, was the work of various hands, and was continued through centuries. It is the most valuable work of the period, for it is history written at the time, and although dry and lifeless, it is not to be despised. Exercising no judgment, nor dramatic power, the writers record great events and lesser transactions in the same style. It is the oldest history of England, and gives us almost all the information we have on the subject of the social life and institutions of our forefathers of that age.

The consideration of this era leads us to the conclusion that English literature began with a high aim, a well-defined idea, and a clear, forcible, and simple utterance. These dignified traits still characterize its best productions, and, notwithstanding many adverse influences, they are too deeply imbedded in the national soul ever to be eradicated.

CHAPTER V.

PERIOD OF IMMATURITY.

Broken English, 1150–1250.

ROM the days of Alfred, English letters declined, and when William of Normandy took his seat on the throne in 1066, he made the ignorance of the prelates whom he found holding sees an excuse for displacing them, and for giving their benefices to more polished scholars from over the channel. We have seen that the preachers of religion were also the promoters of learning, and at some periods they were almost alone in the work. Ecclesiastical power grew steadily and with rapidity after the Conquest. The favorites of William belonged to that body of learned men known as scholastics, who for two centuries, since the days of John Scotus Erigena had been philosophizing about religion.

Scholasticism endeavored to establish a complete system of truth by a train of human reasoning, and under the fostering care of William and his successors, it rose to its greatest influence during the period now under discussion.

While the Norman monarchs fostered scholasticism, they discouraged the culture of the vernacular tongue. This conflict between the speech of the conquerors and the conquered resulted very naturally in the temporary decay of the English. The conflicting languages were of different origin, the one Romanic and the other Teutonic; and the distinctive form of the latter was broken up, and it remained thus disintegrated for nearly two centuries.

Dr. Craik calls this change the first great revolution. It was undoubtedly manifest in the spoken language long before it was displayed in written productions; but at last even literature was affected, and many traits that had previously characterized it were lost.

Before this era the language had been highly inflected, but now, by collision with the Norman speech, which was scarcely inflected at all, our tongue lost its intricate case endings, its numerous verbal inflections, many prefixes and suffixes, and its artificial distinctions of gender. Notwithstanding all this, the change was scarcely perceptible in the root words, which really form the basis of the language.

This great revolution is also apparent in the social and political diction of the nation. At this period Latin was the official language of the clergy, Norman-French that of the court and nobility, and English the speech of the common people. A new social system was organized, and the old English culture went down, as Dr. Craik says, because its natural aliment had failed.

In our last chapter we looked into an ancient hall and heard the gleeman's song. Now we find that he has left us, and quite a different literary character appears on the stage. To realize the change we must imagine ourselves standing before a group of the conventual buildings of the time. We hear the "transient wind whistling through the hollows of the vaulted aisle," and then —

> "All is hushed and still as death. 'Tis dreadful !
> How reverend is the face of this tall pile,
> Whose ancient pillars rear their marble heads,
> To bear aloft its arched and ponderous roof,
> By its own weight made steadfast and immovable,
> Looking tranquillity. It strikes an awe
> And terror on my aching sight ; the tombs
> And monumental caves of death look cold,
> And shoot a chillness to my trembling heart."

By thus revisiting in the imagination a venerable monastic building of the year 1200, we may be aided in getting a vivid idea of the scene. Let us enter that heavy oaken door swinging under the round Norman archway. Walking beneath the massive arcade which formed the cloister, only hesitating a moment to imagine the hooded monks giving their bodies exercise there, we begin to ascend a damp, chill stairway. The beauty of the graceful architecture strikes us pleasantly as we toil upward. The little loop-holes by which we are lighted on our way seem to grow smaller and the passage narrower as we ascend; but it matters not, for we are now admitted to a room with high walls and brighter light.

There is, however, little that is cheerful in the scene before us. The literary men we sought are seated by the rude desks and tables, or are stooping over the great wooden chests that are ranged around the room. If we were to examine these chests we should find in them heaps of precious manuscripts, to which some of the tonsured monks are adding new ones, while others are adorning those already finished.

The tools they use are strange to us. Among them are pens made of reeds and quills, and pencils of hair of various shapes and sizes, and pots of the most brilliant inks — purple and red and violet, — and of gold and silver sizing. The artists are worthy of attention. We find that they belong to the extensive, wealthy, and learned order of Benedictines. To this order belonged Lanfranc, Archbishop of Canterbury, one of the scholastics; and its members especially excelled in the care with which they copied and preserved the valuable manuscripts. The order was wealthy, but we see no appearance of wealth about them, except in the grand and costly architecture of their cheerless building. They are dressed in the flowing black gowns of the order; and the cowl hanging down their backs reveals the bare crowns of their shaven heads, and the circle of hair that fringes them. We must not despise the monks. They worked long and carefully in copying and illustrating their old black-letter rolls. Carefully and lovingly they held their implements day after day, and with an art never surpassed, quietly laid on colors and produced designs which for richness and beauty command our admiration.

We may imagine a monk of note sitting in his great straight-backed chair of oak, with his reed pen or hair pencil in his right hand, and a sharp knife in the left. For days and weeks he has traced the elegant lines around the great character at the head of a chapter, and now we find him rapidly writing the silver letters of one of the Gospels. Now he changes his pencil, and we see him produce one of the sacred names in burnished gold. How reverently it was done! And now he begins a new chapter. The reed is changed again, and we find the monk dipping into the bright red ink to bring out the title in what, even to-day, the printer says is *rubricated.*

Thus, letter by letter, point by point, the monks of the now ruined monasteries copied out, for preservation and transmission to us, a great body of learning which no one else cared for at the time, and which, had it not been for them, would never have come to us. Free from secular cares, they transcribed and preserved books that are now among the choicest treasures of our museums, and they illuminated them with exquisite miniatures, beautiful borderings of flowers, and other designs of original and quaint conception.

LAYAMON'S "BRUT," 1200, is a poetical chronicle of Britain, of about thirty-two thousand lines, written about the year 1200 by a studious parish priest named Layamon. The writer is described as a modest and pious man, living in Worcestershire, a lover of his native land, and one who enjoyed the traditions of its ancient times. In familiar conversational language he relates the tales of Merlin, and King Arthur, of King Lear, and his daughters Gornoille, Ragan, and Cordoille, with other legends of the early days of Britain. Written for the people of a country parish not far from the borders of Wales, this work contains, as we should naturally expect, few words of French origin, and is worthy of study as a specimen of the English of this period.

THE ORMULUM is a simple poetical version of some of the Scripture lessons used in the Church service. The author tells us he was a canon regular of the Order of St. Augustine, and that he composed these Homilies for the spiritual improvement of his countrymen. Only a fragment of the work now remains; but, as it contains some ten thousand long lines, and as there is good reason to believe that near three hundred topics were originally treated, it must have been an immense work. The fragment has, however, great value, being, as is confidently asserted, an autograph of brother Ormin, the author. There is an interesting difference between the form of the *Brut* of Layamon, and the work we are considering. Layamon uses a dialect exhibiting Saxon peculiarities, and brother Ormin's style is marked by a Scandinavian character. Ormin duplicates his consonants when they follow vowels having any other than the name sound. For example he writes for *pane*, p-a-n ; and for *pan*, p-a-n-n, on a principle which obtains to a certain extent to-day, but to which Ormin adheres with rigor. This custom gives to the *Ormulum* an exaggerated appearance of antiquity, of which the following lines will give some idea.

> Nu, brotherr Wallterr, brotherr min
> (*Now, brother Walter, brother mine*)
> Affterr the flaeshes kinde ;
> (*After the flesh's kind*)
> Annd brotherr min i Crisstenndom
> (*And brother mine in Christendom*)
> Thurrh fulluhht and thurrh trowwthe.
> (*Through baptism and through truth*, etc.)

THE ANCREN RIWLE is a prose composition of unknown authorship. Ancren Riwle means *Anchoresses' Rule*, and it is a treatise on the duties of monastic life, addressed to three ladies, who, with their servants, composed a religious community in Dorsetshire. It contains an unusual infusion of words derived from the Latin, which is accounted for by the fact that it was the work of a learned ecclesiastic, and its subject of a religious nature. The spelling is uncouth and irregular.

In the natural and moral worlds night follows day, and death marks the end of life. Periods of energy and faith are succeeded by ages of doubt and sloth. We are now approaching the consideration of one of the dark periods in English literature; but we must not forget that every night brightens into a new day, when the morning sun rises above the eastern horizon; and that it is the hope of man, that though he die and his body be laid among the clods of the valley, he shall live again.

In contemplating the English mind in the annals of a wonderful literature, we notice similar alternations of the brilliant and the sombre. We may justly expect, in the period just before us, some trait pointing to the sun-rising which faith in English manhood and God's providence bids us expect.

CHAPTER VI.

Period of Immaturity.

Dead English, 1250–1350.

HERE is very little to be said about this century. With three languages in England there was, strictly speaking, no English literature, and in fact no national life. English was not a dead language as Greek and Latin are now dead for it was yet used by the common people, and it is only as there was no literature produced in the vernacular that this is called the period of *Dead English*.

In fact the literary productions of any kind were very few during this period. Lord Macaulay points the English nation to the days of King John, one of the meanest of English kings, who ruled from 1199 to 1216, for the origin of its freedom, prosperity, and glory, just as the husbandman points to the seed-time for the origin of the golden harvest of autumn. It was a hopeful period, however, for we have Scriptural authority for saying, "that which is sown is not quickened except it die."

We have remarked the disparagement and disuse of the vernacular by the nobles. Before the period under consideration closed, however, England was separated from Normandy. The conflicting races had become somewhat amalgamated, the interests of the different ranks of the people had been brought into a common field by the over-estimated concessions of the Magna Charta, and the true English spirit reasserted itself. The language now began to be used in literature, as well as in common discourse, even by those who had despised it before. At the beginning of this period, in 1258, King Henry III. issued a proclamation intended for general circulation, which must be accepted as a specimen of the language that was understood by all. It is considered one of the most important relics of early English. A few years after our period closed, in 1362, King Edward III. opened parliament with a speech in the vernacular, which we must consider another concession to the growing influence of the yeomen, who made themselves felt as a power on the brilliant field of Poictiers, — an influence they never afterwards lost.

ROGER BACON, 1214–1294, was a Franciscan friar whose life was one unbroken course of study in science, philosophy, and religion. He was a profound, original thinker, and he opposed the doctrines of those scholastics, who making human reason the basis of religion, had become rationalists. Placing faith in the Scriptures at the foundation of wisdom, and attributing the evils of his time to ignorance of them, he exhorted laymen to read the Bible in the original languages with diligence. But he was three centuries in advance of his time. The world was not ready to accept his doctrine, and for twelve of the later years of his life he languished in prison. If argument were needed to prove that English was dead at this period, it would be enough to say that Roger Bacon, the greatest mind of the age, has left the record of his wisdom solely in the Latin tongue. The mere titles of his works are strong hints of the low estimate he placed upon the vernacular. His chief works are, *Opus Majus*, *Opus Minus*, *Opus Tertium*, *Perspectiva*, *De Speculis*, *De Mirabili Potestate Artis et Naturæ*, and *De Retardandis Senectutis Accidentibus*. These refer generally to science and art.

ROBERT GROSSETESTE, 1175–1253, was a friend and patron of Roger Bacon. After pursuing his studies at Oxford and probably at Paris, he became Bishop of Lincoln. His accomplishments were great and varied, and he wrote a vast number of volumes in Latin. Among them are a book of husbandry, sermons, philosophical treatises, commentaries on Aristotle and Boethius, and some Latin verse.

ROBERT MANNYNG, OF BRUNNE, the dates of whose birth and death are not known, wrote a *Rhyming Chronicle* between 1327 and 1338. It was intended for the learned and unlearned, and, as was usual at the period, for reading aloud. Aiming to have the commonalty, whom he loved, listen to it and be instructed, he wrote in the simplest Saxon English phrase. Among his other works was a *Book of Morals* in rhyme, which was also meant to combine amusement with instruction. Taking the Ten Commandments in order, he illustrated each with doctrine, anecdote, marvel, and moral tale. He then illustrates in a similar style the seven deadly sins, — Pride, Anger, Envy, Sloth, Covetousness, Gluttony, and Lechery. He also treats other subjects, and exhibits the manners of his time in a racy style. He shows us the baron and the rich man plundering the poor; the priest in his lust; the trader and his tricks; the beauty with her powdered face; the chatterers in the church: and again and again the cries of the suffering poor ring through his verse. The list of his subjects brings to mind the solid old parish churches, the vaulted cathedrals, and the now ruined baronial halls of the period, and crowds their vacant chambers with the real life of five centuries ago!

The romances, ballads, and lays of the days of Robert of Brunne bring us to the eve of that revived state of literature which became more and more marked as the brilliant reign of Edward III. progressed, and of which our next chapter treats.

CHAPTER VII.

PEPIOD OF IMMATURITY.

Reviving English, 1350–1558.

WE come now to consider a very interesting period in the history of our literature. Darkness had brooded over the land, and thick darkness had covered the people, as we have seen; but now we are to contemplate a new life. The nation was coming to maturity. The English speech was cultivated more, and why? We must look to history for our answer.

For years after 1340 the French and English were at war. Edward III. was King, and his victories and those of his renowned son, the Black Prince, stirred the British heart, and deepened the love of country. The fact that the victories of Sluys, Cressy, Poictiers, and Calais were to a great extent the work of the English *people* rather than of the nobles, raised the yeomen in their own esteem. This proper patriotism and self-respect, and this military activity, begat an increased literary activity, and an appreciation of the vernacular, which, so far as literature was concerned, had been almost dead for a century.

The period was one of preparation in every country in Europe, a truth which we must keep in view as we consider the authors of the time, but which will be still more apparent when we reach the next chapter. The era begins with the successful wars just mentioned. Before it closed printing had been invented, the Reformation in Germany had been begun by Luther, and the reign of Henry VIII. had ended in England. At its beginning Petrarch and Boccaccio were living in Italy, and Dante had just ceased to sing, while, before it closed, both Ariosto and Tasso had begun and terminated their careers. This revival of intellectual activity was like life from the dead.

The capture of Constantinople by the Turks in 1453, caused the dispersion of a number of men of letters who had resided there. The Medici invited these to Italy, and, with their help, laid the foundations of schools which projected a powerful influence upon the intellectual life of all Europe. Dante and Boccaccio and Petrarch exerted a directing power, during the period under consideration, upon a few English writers, some of whom visited Italy, but it was personal and quite limited. It had had importance, however, as preparing the way for a greater Italian influence to come.

A word must be said here about the effect which translations of the Bible have caused, as exhibited in the domain of literature. A distinguished scholar tells us that the stories of conversion recorded in the Gospels have a liveliness and truth which are felt most strongly by those who know and consider how perfectly new to literature such sketches were when they appeared. "It was by them," he continues, "that the depth and complexity and mystery of the human heart were first brought to light, and their appearance involved a revolution in literature, the results of which are to be traced, not so much in the long barbaric period which followed their diffusion, as in Dante and Shakespeare." The effect of Bible story has already been noticed in Cædmon, singing of God's mercy to the poor and ignorant as he found it there recorded. Again we saw its power in the case of King Alfred, causing all the Gospels to be translated, and at last dying, before his labors to give the Psalms to his loved people were complete. The Archbishop of Canterbury used his time and talents in expounding Scripture doctrines, and gave also the first seven books of the Old Testament to the commonalty. The Venerable Bede translated the Gospel of John, and in 706 Aldhelm the Psalms, which have always been favorites with preacher and people alike. We have in imagination visited the cloisters, and have there seen the Roman Catholic monk of the thirteenth century carefully illuminating costly copies of the Gospels, which his companions had written with equal scrupulousness, on vellum. In the next century we noticed Robert of Brunne illustrating in another way the Ten Commandments, and now we shall have a view of John Wiclif, the keenest schol ar of his day, dividing his time, in the quiet parish of Lutterworth, between visits to the poor, the sick, and the dying, and the heavy labor of translating the whole Bible, for the first time, into the speech of his humblest parishioners. During the period before us we shall notice William Tyndale printing, in Worms in 1525, a version of the New Testament translated from the original Greek, a work which he says he could not find room to do in England. We shall have brought to remembrance, too, good Miles Coverdale, and Bishop Cranmer, who both did much service as translators of the Bible, and Bishop Parker, who, with the help of other scholars, produced the "Bishops' Bible" in 1568, and the Douay Bible which was translated from the Latin text called the Vulgate, though the two last belong to the days of Queen Elizabeth.

Acting, as would appear, on the advice of Roger Bacon, the English people were searching the Scriptures with a will; and we must remember that all this work of translation was done by high officials or prominent members of the Roman Catholic Church. Aside from the religious aspects of this matter, which it is not our province to investigate, the translations of the Bible exerted a powerful influence upon our literature and language. They trained the English mind, and gave it strength, freedom, and cultivation, and they tended to fix the language, and keep it in the forcible and strong state in which it was at the time.

John Mandeville, 1300–1372, is generally considered the first writer of modern English prose. A native of Hertfordshire, he was educated for the medical profession, and became also proficient in natural philosophy and theology. He had no sooner completed his studies than he left England, and for thirty-four years wandered all over the known world. About the year 1356 he returned, and wrote in Latin a Narrative of his Travels, which he subsequently translated into French, and again into English, in order, as he says, "that every man of my nacion may undirstonde it." He was a very credulous, but not a mendacious author, and though he has recorded some of the most extravagantly romantic fables, he makes no effort at exaggeration when writing from his own observation. His book is piquant and was much read, and is a deeply interesting monument of the thought of the period. The author uses a natural style, and incorporates more of the Romanic element than any other writer of the period.

John Wiclif, 1324–1384, was born in Yorkshire in a parish from which he took his name, was thoroughly educated, and in 1372 received from Oxford the degree of Doctor of Divinity, which entitled him to lecture at that University. He lived at the period when the mendicant friars swarmed all over England, and against their abuses, as well as against many other errors of his church, he preached with a holy boldness. In 1377 he was examined as a heretic by order of Pope Gregory XI. in St. Paul's Church. Five papal bulls were issued against him, and in 1382 his works were condemned. But most of the English laymen were with him at first, and at last the humbler priests, taking up his words, trudged all over the land preaching his doctrines wherever they could gather an audience, in church or out of it, in the market-place or at the fair. Silenced at Oxford, and comparatively hidden in the rectory of Lutterworth, Wiclif's influence did not cease. In his retirement he produced the first complete English Bible; then he wrote his *Trialogus*, or conversations on truth, wisdom, and falsehood; then also he wrote a large number of tracts addressed to the people, which were widely read. His tracts are in rugged and sometimes slovenly language. His translation of the Bible is still read with considerable ease.

"VISION OF PIERS PLOWMAN," 1362. This is a work in alliterative verse, written in the strong language of the common people, by an unknown poet. Like Bunyan, the author dreams, and under the guise of allegory not dissimilar to *Pilgrim's Progress*, exhibits the impediments and temptations of life. The author's tone, language, and sentiments, as well as his exhibition of the humor and grumbling so natural to the English, made his work exceedingly popular among the masses, and had probably no small influence in preparing them for the teachings of Wiclif. It presents pictures of social life, describes "Vanity Fair," introduces us to the ecclesiastics, exhibits their vices, and does all with so much directness and detail, that, notwithstanding its great length, it went home to the heart of the humblest to whom it was recited.

GEOFFREY CHAUCER, 1340–1400, was a brother-in-law of John of Gaunt, who was the fourth son of Edward III., and the ancestor of the Tudor line of English sovereigns. He was well educated in English, French, Latin, and Italian, but where and how long he studied is not known, though on slight evidence, it is asserted that he was a member of both Oxford and Cambridge Universities, and studied law at the Inner Temple Court. He was a favorite at the court of Edward III., and had other advantages from his high connections; but, owing to the changes of the times, he was subject to reverses, and for some of his later years lived in retirement, though he had been employed in diplomatic missions to Italy and France. As a consequence he was familiar with foreign customs and style in writing; but, being a hearty Englishman, he only engrafted these on his own stock as the actual wants of our speech demanded. His it was to combine the Romanic and Teutonic elements, and he did it with wonderful tact and sound taste. He was familiar with ancient as well as modern literature, with the fashionable polemic and theological topics of his own day, and was a thorough student of human nature. He respected the Bible and in some degree sympathized with the reformer Wiclif. After a life of varied experience he died in London, and was the first of the poets buried in Westminster Abbey. His reputation rests mainly on his *Canterbury Tales*, a series of humorous and pathetic stories related by a company of persons who are represented to have set out from the Tabard Inn, London, on a pilgrimage to the tomb of Thomas à Becket at Canterbury. If the conception be not original, the details of this work undoubtedly are; for in the description of each of the company, and in the minute account of the incidents of the journey, we plainly see the hand of a master. He brings before us the nun with her beads and neat dress, her gray eyes, small mouth, red lips, her well-proportioned nose, and describes her moral qualities and stately manners. Then we see the mendicant friar, wanton and merry, the miller drunken with ale, the clerk of Oxford, the reve, or bailiff, the knight from the wars of the Crusades, the merchant with forked beard, the franklin, or free-man, with ruddy face and white beard, the haberdasher, carpenter, weaver, and dyer, the sailor, the wife of Bath, the humble and pious par son, the ploughman, who loved God with all his heart, and his neighbor as himself, and the pardoner with smooth yellow flaxen hair hanging over his shoulders, who had come straight from Rome. Each of the pilgrims was to relate two stories going to Canterbury, and two returning, but the poet did not live to complete his design, and only twenty-four tales are included in the work. Among Chaucer's other poetical works, are *The House of Fame, Troilus and Cressida, The Death of Blanche, The Legend of Good Women,* and the *Parlement of Fowls.* They were written with so excellent a choice of words, and in so spirited a manner, that they took a firm hold on the affections of the people, and are capable of charming their readers yet. Chaucer wrote some prose, but his fame rests upon his poetry.

JOHN GOWER, 1320–1408, a friend of Chaucer, is a poet of whose personal history we know very little. He wrote in English, French, and Latin, and lacked his friend's sympathy with the people and admiration of the vernacular. Gower's reputation as an English poet rests upon his *Confessio Amantis,* in which a lover is represented seeking absolution of his confessor, Genius, who refuses to grant it until he has probed the lover to the quick and exposed his weak points. This is carried to the verge of dullness and prosiness, but the moral tone of the work is so elevated that Chaucer called his friend the Moral Gower, a sobriquet which will probably always adhere to him.

Bishop Pecocke, 1390–1460, was a theological writer who opposed the doctrines of Wiclif and the Lollards, but as he admitted that General Councils are fallible, he was not approved by his own party, and was condemned to burn fourteen of his own books at St. Paul's Cross, London, and was afterwards imprisoned. His chief English work is entitled *The Repressor of the too much blaming of the Clergy,* in which, besides the doctrine above, he upholds the Bible as the true rule of faith. His style is popular, lively, clear, and precise.

Sir Thomas Malory, was a knight of whom we know nothing, but that he wrote the famous history of King Arthur, commonly called the *Morte d'Arthur*, about the year 1470. He says he compiled it "oute of certeyn bookes of Frensshe, and reduced it into Englysshe." It was printed by Caxton in 1485 with the title of *The Byrth, Lyfe, and Actes of King Arthur; of His Noble Knyghtes of the Rounde Table,* etc. Though Malory says he compiled this famous work, the English is virtually his own, and as Dr. Craik says, "he shows considerable mastery of expression, his English is always animated and flowing, and in its earnestness and tenderness, occasionally rises to no common beauty and tenderness." The origin of the Round Table romances is involved in impenetrable obscurity. The series comprises six distinct narratives, the first of which is that of the *Sangreal* or *Holy Grail*, which as the holy vessel used by our Saviour at the Last Supper, was, after the crucifixion, preserved by Joseph of Arimathea, and, after many marvelous adventures, brought into Britain. This was probably founded on some religious legend brought from the East by returning crusaders. The second story is that of the enchanter *Merlin*, in which we are introduced to some of the knights of the Round Table, and are made acquainted with the events of Arthur's reign. The third tale relates the adventures of *Lancelot du Lac*. The fourth is the *Queste du St. Greal*, or the search of the Sangreal, in which the prominent figures are Percival, Gawaine, Lancelot, and Galahad, who is finally successful. The next story is the *Morte d'Arthur*, in which we are told of the war which led to Arthur's death. The sixth story, of *Tristan*, called also *Tristram and Iseult*, appears to be of a later date. These romances are assigned to the sixth century, and were partially recorded before the days of Malory. Since his day they have been favorite themes with romancers and poets, as we shall have occasion to see. They have exerted a powerful influence on English literature, and are the subject of the very latest of the poems of Tennyson, the poet laureate of England, published in 1872.

SIR THOMAS MORE, 1480–1535, a friend of the learned and sarcastic Erasmus, once a professor of Greek at Cambridge, was of noble birth, who after studying at Oxford and elsewhere, entered Parliament at about twenty-one years of age. He became conspicuous as a member of Parliament, and under Henry VIII. enjoyed much favor, rising from one degree to another until he finally took the seat on the Chancellor's bench made vacant by the fall of his enemy Cardinal Wolsey. In this high post he was remarkable for his uprightness. His happy home was at Chelsea, now one of the suburbs of London, where, with his loved wife Alice, he used to entertain not only his learned Dutch friend Erasmus, but also clumsy King Henry, and many brilliant literary men of the day. The pleasant days did not last, however; and More's head fell under the headsman's axe, by order of Henry, because the Chancellor would not pronounce the king's marriage with Anne Bullen legal. His principal work in English was a *Life of Richard III.*, of which Hallam says; It "appears to me the first example of good English language; pure and perspicacious, well chosen, without vulgarisms or pedantry." More also wrote a Latin work entitled *Utopia,* which word he constructed from the Greek to mean *nowhere.* It is an original romance, in which he describes a happy island discovered by a supposed companion of Amerigo Vespucci. The writer describes an imaginary and impossible state of society, and is enabled to hit at follies with elegant sarcasm. It is the first of a style of writing in which More had distinguished successors, among whom Dean Swift deserves special mention.

JOHN SKELTON, 1460–1529, was a graduate of Cambridge, and became a tutor of the Duke of York, afterwards Henry VIII. In 1498 he took holy orders, for which he was not fit, and he was suspended by the Bishop of Norwich. He wrote humorous, sarcastic, doggerel rhyme, not lacking in poetical vigor, in which he cudgeled the clergy unmercifully. Erasmus gave him considerable praise for scholarship, calling him the light and ornament of English letters. His chief works are, *Bouge of Court, or Court Diet;* the *Book of Philip Sparrow*, which is an elegy on a sparrow slain by a cat in a nunnery at Norwich, and is comic, imaginative, and original; and *Why come ye not to Court?* a satire of 1300 lines, aimed at Cardinal Wolsey.

HUGH LATIMER, 1472–1555, a famous leader of the Reformation, was born in a Leicestershire farmhouse, was educated at Cambridge, and was one of the earliest English students of Greek. He was in early life a prominent Romanist, but becoming a zealous Protestant, he was burned by Queen Mary, by the side of John Ridley, at Oxford in 1555. His chief productions were sermons, which are fine specimens of homely, unaffected, plain English prose, and have many droll illustrations drawn from local events, and his own experience. He addressed the common people, and his sermons well illustrate the manners of his time and the inner life and thoughts of his hearers.

THOMAS CRANMER, 1489–1556, like Latimer, was educated at Cambridge. He holds the highest rank as a writer among the Reformers, and was influential in establishing the present polity of the Church of England. His great fault was a want of adherence to principle, though at the last he was faithful, and was burned at the stake by Mary. He compiled the *Book of Common Prayer* used now in England, and with slight changes, in America. He superintended a revised translation of the Scriptures, called the "Great Bible," or *Cranmer's Bible.* He also published *Twelve Homilies.*

SIR JOHN CHEKE, 1514–1557, was the first royal professor of Greek at Cambridge, and by his efforts to foster the study of that elegant language, mproved the purity and tone of English prose, in which he was a writer of meritorious style. His only original English work is the *Hurt of Sedition how grievous it is to a Commonwealth.* He wrote learned works in Latin. His writings are grave in style, and he avoided alliteration, and other vices that had become prevalent in literature.

NICHOLAS UDALL, 1506–1564, a Lutheran of some education, head-master at Eton School, (where he was noted for cruel floggings,) was the writer of the first English comedy. It is entitled *Ralph Royster Doyster*, and in it we have a lively picture of London life among the gallants and citizens of the middle class. It possesses a comic spirit and humor without descending to licentiousness or buffoonery, and belongs to a class of writings in which the English nation stands foremost.

ROGER ASCHAM, 1515–1568, was the learned teacher of Elizabeth and Lady Jane Grey. He was the son of a Yorkshire yeoman, a graduate of Cambridge, and a distinguished Greek scholar His chief works are *Toxophilus* and the *Schoolmaster*, which are written in easy conversational prose. In the first the English were taught a lesson in manly sports which they have never forgotten; and in the latter he gave them their first work on education. They are polished, classical, learned, and intelligible now. It is pleasant to look back at this old schoolmaster, reading Latin and Greek with his girlish pupil, the Princess Elizabeth, in 1548; and then, a score of years after, when the princess had become queen, to find her still reading the classics with the old man, or playing *tables* or *shovel-board* with him. When he died Queen Elizabeth exclaimed, "I would rather have thrown ten thousand pounds into the sea than have lost my Ascham!"

Miles Coverdale, 1487–1568, another Yorkshireman, was Bishop of Exeter, and brings us again to the translations of the Bible. Having labored for years, he published a translation in 1535, was engaged upon Cranmer's Bible, and, having been exiled, fled to Geneva, where he helped to produce the *Geneva Bible.*

John Knox, 1505–1572, the son of a Scottish yeoman, was educated at the University of Glasgow, where he took priest's orders. The study of Jerome and Augustine shook his religious opinions, however, and in 1542 he became an avowed and bold reformer. He suffered much persecution, and was an exile in Switzerland for a time, but his boldness was not lessened, and returning to Scotland, he inaugurated a movement which led to the establishment of Presbyterianism in that country. His style is strong, and marked by a want of geniality. He wrote a *History of the Reformation in Scotland*, a pamphlet entitled the *First Blast of the Trumpet against the Monstrous Regiment of Women, Expositions of the Scriptures*, and other tracts. By "Regiment of Women," he meant government of women. It was the time of Mary Stuart in Scotland, Mary Tudor in England, and when those nearest the succession were, in each instance, women.

The period just concluded was to a remarkable extent an era of beginnings.

We considered first Sir John Mandeville, one of the greatest of early English travellers, who is generally styled the first writer of modern English prose. Then, leaving the gay traveller, we saw good old John Wiclif, working in his parsonage at his translation of the Bible, and standing forth as the bright Morning Star of the English Reformation. Next, the author of *Piers Plowman* gave the English the foundation for future allegories.

Geoffrey Chaucer, surrounded by the creations of his fancy, so real as to appear like living men and women, begins the long line of our modern English poets. From the mists of the ages now Sir Thomas Malory just emerges, to hand us his carefully treasured book, — the first connected account of King Arthur and his knights. He no sooner appears than he is gone, and in his place Sir Thomas More comes forward, dressed in his Chancellor's robes. He leaves us a volume telling of a land that is nowhere, a land of ideal loveliness and of bliss the world shall never see. "Now," he says, "you may look for Utopias; and your authors will henceforth know how to write satirical romance."

We saw Cranmer perish at the stake, but it was not until he had given England her Prayer Book, and her Church Polity. And now Nicholas Udall crowds himself upon our view, and with mock gravity lays before us *Ralph Royster Doyster*, and we recognize the first English comedy. The patriarch advancing now is Roger Ascham, holding in his still sinewy grasp the first treatise on education, and his argument for manly sports.

Before the curtain drops we find ourselves walking down the High Street of Edinburgh. Just as we pass the Heart of Mid-lothian we encounter a crowd, and, looking upward, see a venerable form at a little pulpit-like window that juts over the pavement. The appearance of the crowd, and the words we now and then catch, tell us the old man is preaching. Listening again we hear the Monstrous Regiment of Women denounced, and then we remember that it was John Knox who first gave Presbyterianism to Scotland!

CHAPTER VIII.

MATURE ENGLISH.

The Italian Influence, 1558–1649.

HE period before us is often called the *Age of Elizabeth*, and the *Golden Age*, either of which terms is appropriate. It includes, however, not only the reign of England's greatest queen, but also those of her successors, James I. who died in 1625, and Charles I. who was beheaded in 1649. The first half of Elizabeth's reign is not marked by the production of works that should give the period the high distinction it has received.

At the beginning of the era just concluded there had been a notable increase of literary life, but the activity did not continue throughout the period. The fifty years before the accession of Elizabeth were crowded with exciting changes.

Henry VIII. began to reign in 1509, at the age of eighteen. He was a monarch of caprices, which were exhibited in other relations as well as in his dealings with his wives. At the time of his accession, Thomas Wolsey was Dean of Lincoln, having previously been one of the chaplains of Henry VII., and to him, for various reasons, the young king looked for advice. Wolsey cultivated his esteem and obtained many preferments, but differing with him on the subject of Queen Catherine's divorce, Henry charged his favorite with high treason. Wolsey was disgraced, and would have been executed, had he not died at Leicester Abbey, to which place he had fled for refuge. Sir Thomas More took Wolsey's place, but was subsequently beheaded, a martyr to the royal caprice. Thomas Cranmer, the third favorite, outlived his royal master, but it was only to perish in the reign of his daughter Mary.

Among the other events were Henry's defiance of the Pope of Rome, his wars with France, the demolition of the monasteries and convents, terrible persecutions of papists, hangings, burnings, and beheadings, and such violations of the liberties guaranteed by the Magna Charta as no English sovereign was ever before guilty of. The people were in terror.

The short reign of Edward VI. was a season of comparative quiet; but when his sister Mary came to the throne there was a great change. Inaugurating her accession by the execution of Lady Jane Grey, she carried on the government in the spirit of the Tudor family, to which she belonged, and her reign was marked by that despotic use of power of which the Stuarts afterwards reaped the fruits.

Notwithstanding the delirium of joy with which Elizabeth's accession, or rather the death of Mary, was received, the early years of her reign were by no means undisturbed. The painful circumstances connected with the imprisonment of Mary Stuart, ending with her execution in 1587, the executions caused by the enforcement of the act of Supremacy, and the loss of their livings suffered by many clergymen of the Church of England who could not in conscience submit to the Act of Uniformity, — these exciting affairs so engrossed public attention that small interest was manifested in letters.

By degrees, however, quiet was restored, and men began to breathe more freely. There was universal progress, new knowledge was eagerly received, and literary topics assumed greater importance.

Nor was this activity apparent only in England. In his Polish observatory Copernicus had already concluded the observations which led to the publication in 1543 of his great work, "On the Revolution of the Heavenly Bodies." Cortez had just before conquered the rich kingdom of Mexico for his sovereign Charles V., and it was the era of the formation of the Dutch Republic, as well as of the revolt of the Moors in Spain. It was the period of the Spanish Armada, of the voyages of Sir Francis Drake, of the increase of England's naval power, of the introduction of tobacco and of potatoes, of the great reformation of Luther in Germany, of the

Council of Trent, and of the revival of arts, sciences and literature throughout Europe.

New worlds, new peoples, new wealth, everything appeared new, or in a new phase, and there arose that galaxy of lights in the literary firmament which pale the rays, as well of those who went before, as of all who have since risen.

Another influence contributed also to mark the line between immaturity and maturity, than which no other was more potent. This was the printer's press, which had been introduced in the fifteenth century, and was now showing its fruits in a more fixed language. Before this time every writer wrote and spelled too much as he pleased, without rule, and not even observing uniformity in different parts of the same work. Now, when one man published many books, the need of uniformity was more apparent, and since he circulated many copies his example became a guide to others, and the form as well as the style of our language grew more fixed.

Sir Philip Sidney, 1554–1586, whom Queen Elizabeth called the jewel of her dominions, was of illustrious family, being a nephew of Robert Dudley, Earl of Leicester. After receiving a careful education at Oxford and Cambridge, he entered public life, and became the pet of the people as well as the pride of the queen. He died at the age of thirty-two from the effect of a wound received in a battle fought to aid the Protestants of the Netherlands against the Spanish Romanists. Sidney wrote little or nothing for publication, and yet, by his posthumous works, exerted a powerful influence upon the intellectual spirit of his age, and ranks among the best writers of the time. His fame rests principally upon *The Arcadia*, a heroic romance, written at Wilton, the seat of his sister, the Countess of Pembroke; and the *Defence of Poesie*, which is one of the earliest pieces of English criticism. In the latter work the author, who was sensible of the genius often concealed in rude legends and ancient ballads, shows the advantages of the cultivation of imaginative literature, which the growing Puritanism of the age was disparaging.

CHRISTOPHER MARLOWE, 1563–1593, the greatest dramatist before Shakespeare, was the son of a shoemaker. After his graduation at Cambridge, he wrote *Tambourlaine the Great*, *Dr. Faustus*, the *Jew of Malta*, and *Edward II.*, which are full of dramatic incidents and poetic beauty, though they are criticized as in parts bombastic, extravagant, and sometimes licentious. Marlowe died at the age of thirty, being killed in a disreputable quarrel.

EDMUND SPENSER, 1553–1599, was some years older than Marlowe, and like him a graduate of Cambridge. He was a friend of Sidney, and a courtier of Elizabeth, but we naturally associate him with Ireland, for the queen granted him three thousand acres in the county of Cork, as pay for services rendered her. His masterpiece is *The Faerie Queen*, an unfinished allegorical poem. It is rich in expression, and is one of the most luxurious and melodious of our descriptive poems. In it the author shows the fruit of his study of *Piers Plowman* and Chaucer, and since the days of the latter of these writers, none so graced our literature as Spenser, and after him no equal arose until Shakespeare appeared. *The Faerie Queen* was to have consisted of twelve books, with King Arthur as the hero, but only six were completed. Of these the first is the gem. It recounts the adventures of a knight of the court of Gloriana, the Faerie Queen whom Arthur loves. In it we find the Redcross knight Holiness, as a militant Christian seeking the hand of Una, a beautiful woman representing Truth. The knight is seduced by Duessa, Falsehood, and is reduced almost to despair, when by the intervention of Una, and the help of Faith, Hope, and Charity, he is rescued. In the other books the adventures of other knights, representing Temperance, Chastity, Friendship, Justice, and Courtesy, are recounted, but they do not equal the first. These stories have been likened to Tennyson's *Idyls of the King*. Among Spenser's other works are *The Shepherd's Calendar*, *The Tears of the Muses* *The Ruins of Time*, and many others.

RICHARD HOOKER, 1553–1600, was a divine who adhered to the Established Church as against the Puritans, who, since the days of Cranmer, had not ceased to oppose the governmental religion. According to Hallam, Hooker was the first to adorn prose with the images of poetry, and though some critics object to the great length of his sentences, the best agree in admiring the beauty and dignity of his style. The latest essay on this author is a discriminating critique in Whipple's *Literature of the Age of Elizabeth.* Hooker is the ablest champion his church ever had, and his *Ecclesiastical Polity*, on which his fame now mainly rests, is a monument of close reasoning supported by the most extensive learning.

JOHN LYLY, 1553–1601, is distinguished as the author of *Euphues*, and *Euphues and his England*, works immensely popular in the author's day, but which were out of print and neglected for two hundred and thirty-two years, that is, from 1636 to 1868. The works treat of friendship, love, education, and religion, and their fastidious pedantry and effort after antithesis have given the term *Euphuism* to our language.

WILLIAM SHAKESPEARE, 1564–1616, the brightest in the long line of immortal names that gild the pages of English literature, was born and died at Stratford-upon-Avon, and there he lies buried. This and very little more we know of his life. Like the records in the Scriptures of the life of some Hebrew worthy, it is not at all satisfying to curiosity. He was a companion of Ben Jonson, Sir Walter Raleigh, and others in their revels at the Mermaid and Falcon inns, and a man of social, if not of gayer habits of life. Coleridge described him as of oceanic mind, by which he intended to express the same idea of multitudinous unity, as when in another place he called him thousand-souled. In their grasp, variety, and moral teachings, as well as in aptness to promote spiritual strength, the works of Shakespeare stand among the world's books second only to the Bible. One chief reason for this is that of all books the Scriptures exerted the greatest formative and guiding influence on the mind of the dramatist, a fact that has been admirably pointed out by the Rev. Charles Wordsworth in an English work entitled *The Bible and Shakespeare*, the fruit of much love for and deep study of each book. The Holy Bible and the wisdom of Shakespeare have moulded many of the strongest minds of the last three hundred years. Shakespeare's works are believed by some to contain more actual wisdom than the whole body of English learning, of course leaving mere science out of the question. He wrote thirty-seven plays — tragedies, comedies, and historical plays, among which in their classes, the following are probably the greatest: *Macbeth, King Lear, Romeo and Juliet, Hamlet,* and *Othello*

Midsummer Night's Dream, *As You Like it*, and *Merchant of Venice*, and *Richard III.*, *Henry V.*, *King John*, *Coriolanus*, and *Julius Cæsar*. Some authors may be said to equal Shakespeare in a particular point, but none possess his wonderful power of searching out and exhibiting the intimate workings of the human heart; and it may safely be asserted that he leaves far behind him not only all dramatists, but all writers of fiction.

THE AUTHORIZED VERSION OF THE BIBLE, 1611, is a translation made by order of King James I., during the years 1607–1611, by a body of forty-seven divines. They were directed to take the Bishops' Bible printed in 1568, and based upon Cranmer's, as the foundation of their work. The labor was conducted in a spirit of affectionate veneration and carefulness, and the result was a book unequaled among literary works for its English, and embodying sublime eloquence, magnificent poetry, beautiful imagery, and clear, impressive history. The translators published an address "To the Reader," which was originally included in their volume. In it they give a history of the text, and of the former translations, from which the following passage is taken: "Truly wee neuer thought from the beginning, that we should neede to make a new Translation, nor yet to make of a bad one a good one; but to make a good one better, or out of many good ones, one principall good one, not iustly to be excepted against; that hath bene our indeauour, that our marke." They say that they "have set a varietie of sences in the margine," — a practice which they support by argument, and they add a number of items of information about their work which are well worthy of perusal. As a philological power this translation has not had its equal, apart from its spiritual importance.

FRANCIS BACON, 1561–1626, Lord Verulam, next to William Shakespeare was the brightest star of this period. Deeply involved during his whole life in the intricacies of public business, he found time, strange as it may appear, to produce his immortal works. Forever famous as a writer on philosophy, his *Essays* also stand among the most finished works in pure English literature, being characterized by weighty thoughts, sound judgment, and elevated morality. While the language is spoken, these brief essays will continue to furnish food for thought, while his philosophical writings may be comparatively neglected in the advance of modern science. He is called the founder of the Baconian philosophy, or the Inductive system, for though it was applied before his time, he did more than any one, by his eloquence and brilliancy, to direct attention to that which was overlooked. He was endowed with one of the most capacious and profound intellects ever possessed by man, and also with a wonderfully fertile imagination. His works are all reflective, and in a certain aspect poetical, and yet no prose writer was ever so concise as Bacon. His chief works are *Essays*, *The State of Europe*, *History of Henry VII.*, *The Dignity and Advancement of Learning*, and the *Novum Organum.*

BEAUMONT and FLETCHER, were two dramatists who wrote together, as was then somewhat the fashion, and as we have now examples in Erckmann-Chatrian in France. John Fletcher was born in 1576, and Francis Beaumont in 1586. Educated at Cambridge and Oxford, they died, Beaumont in 1615, and Fletcher in 1625. They wrote with so intimate a union, that their separate contributions cannot be determined, and were popular, not so much on account of their scholarship as for their brilliancy and humor. Their numerous plays are marred by vulgarity and grossness. Among them are, *Rule a Wife and Have a Wife*, *The Woman-Hater*, *The Faithful Shepherdess*, *The Two Noble Kinsmen*, *The Wild Goose Chase*, *Wit without Money*, and *The Coronation.*

MICHAEL DRAYTON, 1563–1631, was poet laureate in 1626, and wrote voluminously, with originality, but without the truly great comprehensive spirit of a poet. One of his works, *Poly-Olbion*, is a minute topographical description of England in thirty thousand wearisome lines. *The Barons' Wars* is a metrical chronicle; and *Nymphidia* is a fairy poem, which has been well styled one of the most deliciously fanciful creations in the language.

JOHN DONNE, 1573–1631, was of Welsh extraction, a Romanist by birth, but after studying the points of difference between Romanists and Protestants, he changed his faith, and attained prominence as Dean of St. Paul's, and as a foremost man of letters. After a youth of gayety, he embraced the clerical profession, and became remarkable for his deep piety. His great intellectual powers were devoted to the production mainly of sermons and poems. The former have been highly extolled by Izaak Walton, one of his biographers, who ardently admired his friend Donne, but, in the calmer judgment of Hallam, there is not much in them worthy of being rescued from oblivion. Mr. Hallam further says: "His learning he seems to have perverted, in order to cull every impertinence of the fathers and schoolmen, their remote analogies, their strained allegories, their technical distinctions; and to these he has added much of a similar kind from his own fanciful understanding." The poems of Dr. Donne are equally grotesque with his prose. They are crowded with far-fetched similes, painful puns, and extravagant metaphors, and these traits, though giving them temporary popularity, caused them long to be neglected. A discriminating taste, however, now finds in them many gems of much poetic beauty, which embody elevating conceptions. His chief works are, *Epithalamia*, *Metempsychosis, or the Progress of the Soul*, *Funeral Elegies*, *Divine Poems*, and *Songs and Sonnets*. He also wrote a book in vindication of suicide, entitled *Biathanatos*, published in 1651, in which the arguments are obscurely stated, and of which Mr. Hallam says: "No one would be induced to kill himself by reading such a book, unless he were threatened with another volume." Dr. Donne is said to have founded what Dr. Johnson called the Metaphysical School of Poetry, the authors in which appeared to aim to make their meaning as difficult to be found out as possible, using all the resources of great learning to conceal thought. Professor Reed says of it, that "It was deemed the perfection of poetry so to entangle every poetic image or impulse in a maze of scholastic allusions, in forced and arbitrary turns of thought, paradoxes, antitheses, quaintnesses, subtleties, that the reader's chief pleasure must have been the exercise of a correspondent and inappropriate ingenuity in discovering the path of the labyrinth. It could have been no more than the negative satisfaction of unraveling a riddle. . . . The irredeemable sin of this school of poetry was its sacrifice of nature, and consequently of poetic truth. . . . It demands not so much thought as shrewdness, acuteness, ingenuity, intellectual dexterity; or perhaps it would describe it more justly, as well as more favorably, to say that it demands thought and nothing but thought, — no imagination, no passion, which are the life of real poetry."

George Herbert, 1593–1632, was a younger brother of the deistical writer, Lord Edward Herbert of Cherbury, with whose life and character he is so remarkably contrasted. An impartial judgment of his literary merit is difficult to obtain. His poetry is devotional, pure, and forcible, but is marred by the quaintness and fantastic imagery of the metaphysical school to which he belonged. The pure life of George Herbert, his gentleness and unction, and the beauty of a few of his less faulty poems, have given him a greater reputation than many of the poets of his school. He wrote *The Temple*, in verse, and *A Priest to the Temple*, in prose. The former is a collection of sacred poems, among which are the lines on "Virtue" beginning —

> "Sweet day, so cool, so calm, so bright,
> The bridal of the earth and sky."

It also contains the familiar verses on "Sunday," beginning —

> "O day most calm, most bright,
> The fruit of this, the next world's bud."

Ben Jonson, 1574–1637, who first drew the scenes for comedy from English home life, is by common consent accorded the position nearest to

Shakespeare, of whom he was a close companion, and with whom and kindred wits he was wont to enjoy the historic meetings at the Mermaid Inn. At the age of twenty-two he produced his first comedy, *Every Man in his Humor*, which Hallam says is "an extraordinary monument of early genius, in what is seldom the possession of youth, — a clear and unerring description of human character, various and not extravagant beyond the necessities of the stage." Jonson was an assiduous worker, and it may well be doubted that he cherished envy toward his elder companion, Shakespeare, or that he indulged in wine-bibbing and gluttony to the extent sometimes attributed to him. He was bluff and hearty, a true son of England, was a brilliant wit, and appears to have been surrounded by an appreciative circle of talented persons, who were charmed by his society. His characters do not always present us representatives of large classes of society, but often exhibit peculiar specimens which in the author's day assumed prominence. Among his other works are, *Every Man out of his Humor*, *Cynthia's Revels*, *Sejanus*, *Catiline*, *Epicene*, and *The Alchemist*.

JOHN FORD, 1586–1640, was the last of the original dramatists of this period. He appears to have been a melancholy man of retiring habits, and his writings are marked by pathos, intensity, and sweetness, though deficient in variety. His powers are best shown in his tragedy of *The Broken Heart.*

JOHN SELDEN, 1584–1654, is known to the present generation as the author of *Table Talk*, a volume first published by his amanuensis thirty years after his death. He was, however, the author of numerous historical and antiquarian works, and one of the most learned of the graduates of Oxford at the time. He made himself unpopular with the authorities by favoring the people in their struggles against the usurpations of king and clergy. His funeral sermon was preached by Archbishop Usher, and his books were given by his executors to the Bodleian library.

In the freedom of its thought and the boldness of its utterance, the literature of this era proclaims the influence of the Reformation. It exhibits some of the benefits of the intellectual enfranchisement effected by the liberator of modern thought, whose power was felt in other countries besides Germany, and in other realms besides those of morals and religion.

The age of Elizabeth gave us the charming romance and criticism of Sidney, the exquisite verse of Spenser, the close logic of Hooker, the wonderful philosophy of Bacon, the fantastic images of Donne, the quaint verse of Herbert, the hearty humor of Jonson, the universal genius of Shakespeare, and the sublime eloquence of our Bible!

CHAPTER IX.

MATURE ENGLISH.

The Puritan Influence, 1649–1660.

ON Tuesday, January 30, 1649, King Charles I. was publicly beheaded in front of Whitehall Banqueting-house. It was a place that had witnessed many strange scenes, — that old palace of Whitehall. There Henry VIII. and Anne Bullen were married. Bishop Latimer preached in the court once, while King Edward VI. sat at a window to hear him. Sir Thomas Wyatt's Kentish rebels "shotte divers arrowes into the courte" in 1554, thereby terrifying the fair dames about Bloody Mary. There Queen Elizabeth kept her library of Greek, Latin, Italian, and French books; and there, in 1600, she appointed a Frenchman to do "feates upon a rope in the conduit court, the bear, the bull, and the ape to be bayted in the tilt court, and solemn dawncing on Wednesday," and in the great gallery the same virgin queen received the Speaker and the House of Commons, when they came to "move her grace to marriage." In the King's bedchamber Guy Fawkes was examined, and taken thence to the Tower. There were performed some of those old masques that Ben Jonson loved to compose. But a change came — the old building was destroyed, a new one erected, — and it was not long after Charles stepped out of an upper window to the scaffold, that Oliver Cromwell assembled his "Barebones Parliament," as it was called, in the new Council Chamber, and there the Protector died too, in 1658. There John Milton acted as Cromwell's Latin secretary; and there came Edmund Waller, Andrew Marvel, and sometimes a young man, afterward better known, — John Dryden.

The temporary triumph of the Puritans over the Cavaliers is marked by this change of inmates at Whitehall. For a hundred years almost, the struggle had been going on in the kingdom; and on that Tuesday afternoon when King Charles was beheaded, the Commons ordered that the weekly post be stayed until the next morning at ten of the clock, in order that news of the crowning act might be spread throughout the land as speedily as possible. A night of distress intervened, for every one was astonished, curious to know what next would happen, and anxious for his own personal safety or popularity. The beneficed clergy, members of the university, and civil officers, were in a state of fear, but it was unnecessary, for, with the exception of five prominent royalists, they were to be treated with moderation.

The change at court exerted an unavoidable influence upon literature. The influence of the Puritan had long been felt, but now that the Cavalier was obliged to take a place in the background, the opposite party was left free to develop itself as well in literature as in morals and politics.

We have limited the period to the eleven years of the Commonwealth, or the interregnum between the execution of Charles I. and the Restoration of Charles II., in 1660, when new fashions were introduced at court, and a new spirit came over authors as well as people. We must therefore speak not only of those who lived and wrote during the period as defined, but also of some others whose productions were moulded or modified by Puritan principles. Not a few of these appeared in their greatest glory after the Restoration, when the Puritans were hated and hunted from their homes.

We should expect now to find prose developed more than poetry, for while the latter is the channel through which highly wrought emotion is expressed, discussions upon human rights, civil government, and religious subjects, are more naturally carried on in prose. The earnestness and power with which the Puritan authors wielded the native speech has left an impress upon our prose which can never be effaced. The period is, however, not entirely destitute of verse, for the Puritans found lyrical poetry well adapted to the purposes of song in Christian worship, and the sublime Milton has left us the great English epic, in a *Paradise Lost*, while some Cavaliers still sung their love-ditties, praised the banished king and queen, or ridiculed the face, fashion, and tones of the "town's new teacher"—the Puritan.

FRANCIS QUARLES, 1592–1644, was an ardent royalist, but his writings have a strong religious cast, and are much tinged with Puritanism and pious asceticism. He used the conceited and extravagant style of the period, which gave his poems popularity at first, but has caused them to be neglected since. His chief poems are, *Divine Emblems*, *Job Militant*, *The History of Queen Esther*, and *The Feast of Worms.*

WILLIAM BROWNE, 1590–1645, is known chiefly as the writer of *Britannia's Pastorals*, *The Inner Temple Masque*, and *The Shepherd's Pipe.* These poems, written somewhat in the style of Spenser, combine pastoral poetry with allegory, are marked by some grace, and exhibit some facility of thought and originality of expression.

WILLIAM DRUMMOND, 1585–1649, was the first Scotsman who wrote good English, and was also one of the most graceful poets of the time. He lived at Hawthornden, a lovely spot in the vicinity of Edinburgh, near Roslyn Castle. The poetic spirit of the romantic scenery of the glens and crags and beautiful banks of the river Eske seems to have entered his soul and to have been breathed out in his verse. His chief works are, *Flowers of Sion*, *Wandering Muses, or the River Forth Feasting*, and *Sonnets*. He was a friend of Ben Jonson, who visited him in his Scotch home, and of other English authors. Milton is said to have copied some of his images.

THOMAS FULLER, 1608–1661, was an active royalist politician, a prominent theological writer of euphuistic style, and is said to have made more jokes in writing than any other man. He wrote *Essays*, *Tracts*, *Sermons*, *The Worthies of England*, *Church History of Britain*, *The Holy and Profane State*, and the *History of the Holy War*. His writings abound in lofty morality, deep feeling, eloquent pathetic passages, and romantic stories, and he is reputed one of the truest and greatest wits who ever lived.

ABRAHAM COWLEY, 1618–1667, was also a royalist, of good education, who rose to a sudden popularity which has not increased in the lapse of time. This is accounted for by the fact that he is a representative of the so-called metaphysical school of poets. His principal works are, *Miscellanies*, *Anacreontics*, *Pindaric Odes*, *The Mistress*, and *The Davideis*. The last is an unfinished epic, which was intended to have recounted the glories of the King of Israel, a design which it is supposed the author relinquished with the feeling that Milton would produce a greater Scriptural poem than he could. Cowley's verse is forced and unnatural. His prose is simple, manly, and rhythmical.

JEREMY TAYLOR, 1613–1667, whose works in vellum and gold still grace the boudoir and the cabinet, was the greatest divine of the age, a man of apostolic sublimity and sweetness of character. His *Liberty of Prophesying* was the first famous plea for tolerance in religion. It is remarkable as having been published just at the end of the Commonwealth by an episcopalian and a royalist, and illustrates the influence of the Puritans on those outside of their own body. His other chief works are *Holy Living and Dying*, *Life of Christ*, *The Golden Grove*, and *Sermons*. Taylor has been called both the Shakespeare and the Spenser of divines, and he undoubtedly resembles the latter author in his prolific fancy, musical arrangement, prolonged and poetical descriptions, and in his musings, metaphors, and enthusiasm. His highly ornamental style is not exempt from the fantastic blemishes which characterize the age.

GEORGE WITHER, 1588–1667, is generally classed among the Puritan writers, notwithstanding his reputation as a poet was made before he became identified with that body. His life was one of great activity and reverses. He was at one time a

Major-General under Cromwell. His chief works are, *Abuses Stript and Whipt*, *Shepherds' Hunting*, *Mistress of Philarete*, *Emblems*, and a poem on *Christmas*. The second of these was composed in prison, into which he was thrown for writing the first, and in view of these circumstances it is a remarkable work. He wrote excellent English, but critics have been very much divided as to his merits as a poet and a man.

SIR WILLIAM DAVENANT, 1605–1668, was an energetic royalist, a great admirer of Shakespeare, and reminds us that we are approaching the era of the French influence. During the Protectorate he was banished to France, and at the Restoration he aided in the revival of the theatre, which had been closed since 1648. His principal poem was heroic and chivalrous, but of little merit, and was written in France. It is entitled *Gondibert*.

JOHN MILTON, 1608–1674, is a poet whose works are as current now as they were in his own days. He was the son of an ardent republican, of old and gentle family, and from his early years was set apart to the service of patriotism and letters. His education was carefully conducted at home, at St. Paul's School, London, and finally at Cambridge. His remarkable life has very properly been divided into three natural periods. The first extends from 1623 to 1640, during which he produced his *Ode to the*

Nativity, the *Masque of Comus*, the pastoral elegy of *Lycidas*, the descriptive poems, *L'Allegro*, and *Il Penseroso*, and his *Sonnets*. Those gave the young author a high position among the poets of the nation, and charmed their readers by the tokens of genius, the graceful eloquence, and refined and courtly emotions they embody. Of the sonnets are one *To the Nightingale*, and another on the *Massacre of the Piedmontese Protestants*. They all relate either to religion, patriotism, or domestic affection. The second period of Milton's life extends from 1640 to 1660, during which, being involved in political and religious controversy, he produced his marvellous prose writings. His language is forcible, eloquent, and grand, notwithstanding the inverted forms of expression and the words of Latin origin which he used. Among his writings at this time are, *Of Reformation in England*, *The Reason of Church Government urged against Prelaty*, *Apology for Smectymnuus*, *Doctrine and Discipline of Divorce*, *Areopagitica*, *A Speech for the Liberty of Unlicensed Printing*, and *The Likeliest Form to remove Hirelings out of the Church*. These contain many eloquent passages, full of imagination, grandeur, and exhibitions of the author's intense love of liberty. Notwithstanding all, it is undisputed that Milton's prose is not of the best nor most idiomatic. We are brought now to the third and last period of Milton's life, extending from 1660 to 1674. He appears again as a poet, not in the exuberant fancy of youth, but in the matured richness of age. His writings of this era are, *Paradise Lost*, *Paradise Regained*, and *Samson Agonistes*. The first is undoubtedly the greatest epic poem in the language, and is only comparable with the three other epics of Greece, Rome, and modern Italy. Homer, Virgil, Dante, Milton, are names that stand alone on the world's record. Mr. Shaw says, "As the antique world produced two great epic types, so did Christianity, — Dante and Milton. Dante represents the poetic side of Catholic, Milton of Protestant Christianity; Dante its infancy, its age of faith and heroism; Milton its virile age, its full development and exaltation. Dante is the Christian Homer, Milton the Christian Virgil. If the predominant character of Homer be vivid life and force, and of Virgil majesty and grace; that of Dante is intensity, and of Milton is sublimity." In his tragedy of *Samson Agonistes*, Milton embodies his own blindness, sufferings, and resignation to God's will, in a touching manner, and it fittingly closes his sublime career.

Edmund Waller, 1605–1687, was one of those whose personal character covers them with infamy, while their writings are admired for their grace, originality, beauty, and good sense. His father was a gentleman of large estates, and his mother was a sister of John Hampden. The latter circumstance drew him toward the republicans, and he greatly distinguished himself on the popular side. But as he was equally ready to flatter Charles II. or to praise Cromwell, he is now considered a mean-souled man. His poems are graced with smoothness and polish, and he ranks high as an improver of English verse. His principal writings are *Miscellaneous Poems*, containing his *Panegyric to the Lord Protector*, and *Amatory Verses.*

RALPH CUDWORTH, 1617–1688, was a learned divine and philosopher, who wrote *The True Intellectual System of the Universe*, a blow at the atheism of his day. He was Hebrew professor at Cambridge, and his work is a vast storehouse of learning, and is unrivaled as a display of subtle and far-reaching speculation.

JOHN BUNYAN, 1628–1688, was one of the most remarkable religious writers of any age. He was a tinker, and the son of a tinker, and yet he is known wherever our language is spoken, as the author of an allegory, the most simple, the most life-like, the most original and imaginative, the most captivating and affecting in the range of literature. Bunyan's *Pilgrim's Progress* is popular now — was popular when first published — with the aged and the young, the learned and the unlearned, the prince and the peasant. The author knew little of books, but he studied our grand English Bible, and was saturated with its spirit as well as words. He was indeed a man of one book, but that, the Book of Books This gave him power, and as Lord Macaulay says, "Bunyan is as decidedly the first of allegorists, as Demosthenes is the first of orators, or Shakespeare the first of dramatists."

RICHARD BAXTER, 1615–1691, was a voluminous writer, and one of the most eminent non-conformist divines of the day. During the civil war he sympathized with Parliament, but being a zealous advocate of regular government in Church and State, he disapproved Cromwell's usurpation. His life was devoted to the promotion of piety and good morals, and his great merits were acknowledged by his distinguished friends, Dr. Isaac Barrow, Bishop Wilkins, and Sir Matthew Hale. He is reputed the author of near two hundred books, three of which were large folios, but none of them, excepting *The Saint's Everlasting Rest*, and *A Call to the Unconverted*, are much read. Like Bunyan, he used good, strong, homely English, and his works abound in choice and glowing imagery, and passages of hearty eloquence.

A glance over this chapter will render our progress manifest, and will prove that the period of the Commonwealth was not without its effect upon our literature. We first saw, as we opened it, the figure of quaint Francis Quarles bearing to our gathering stores of literary riches his *Emblems*, *Job Militant*, and *Feast of Worms*, and not far behind was his younger friend Cowley, asking us to look at his *Odes*, and only exhibiting his unfinished *Davideis* to tell us that he had left the field of epic poetry for another to occupy. Then, away up in Scotland, among the picturesque scenery of Hawthornden, we saw burly old Ben Jonson walking by the river Eske, admiring nature somewhat, but praising in higher terms the verse of the friend by his side, William Drummond, the first of his people to write good English.

It was quite another picture when the witty Fuller appeared, cracking his jokes with his learned, fanciful, and somewhat younger companion Jeremy Taylor. Still younger was the eminent Hebrew professor Cudworth, who was piling up the vast stores of learning which have made his *Intellectual System* so formidable to ordinary readers, and so astonishing to the learned.

There were three others who always hold the attention of one who studies the days of the Puritan rule. Looking into Whitehall we saw John Milton acting as Latin secretary to the stern Roundhead who then occupied the home of the cavalier king. Had we followed him when he left that hall, we should have found the politician reassuming the poet's pen which he had dropped to become secretary.

Had we gone forty-five miles from Whitehall in 1660, we might have met in the common jail at Bedford, the most accomplished allegorist of all history. There he was confined for the twelve years that followed, and there he wrote his *Pilgrim's Progress*, for his jailer was kind-hearted, and allowed him pen, ink, and paper, and for reading, *Foxe's Book of Martyrs* and the *Bible.*

As we closed the chapter, we had before us the frail body of that voluminous writer who gave us *The Saint's Everlasting Rest.* Let us look into the famous Guildhall of London; we may see him again for a moment. It is the room in which the Lord Mayors have annually feasted their sovereigns for two hundred years. As we look down toward the great gothic window, we see the bloated drunkard who became so celebrated as Judge Jeffreys, sitting in the midst of a group of lawyers and jurymen. Before them, frail, feeble, and helpless, stands Baxter trying to make himself heard. But all his efforts are fruitless. The brutal judge roars "Richard, Richard! Dost thou think we will let thee poison this court? Thou hast written books enough to load a cart, and every book as full of sedition as an egg is full of meat!" We hear the jury meekly render a verdict of "guilty," — we ask not of what, — and, as the officers lead their unresisting prisoner to jail, we retire and breathe more freely as we become conscious that we are in the atmosphere of the nineteenth century!

CHAPTER X.

Mature English.

The French Influence, 1660–1700.

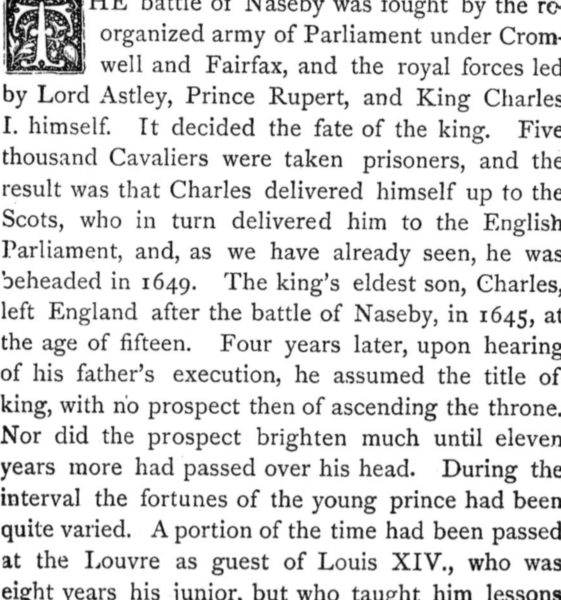

THE battle of Naseby was fought by the reorganized army of Parliament under Cromwell and Fairfax, and the royal forces led by Lord Astley, Prince Rupert, and King Charles I. himself. It decided the fate of the king. Five thousand Cavaliers were taken prisoners, and the result was that Charles delivered himself up to the Scots, who in turn delivered him to the English Parliament, and, as we have already seen, he was beheaded in 1649. The king's eldest son, Charles, left England after the battle of Naseby, in 1645, at the age of fifteen. Four years later, upon hearing of his father's execution, he assumed the title of king, with no prospect then of ascending the throne. Nor did the prospect brighten much until eleven years more had passed over his head. During the interval the fortunes of the young prince had been quite varied. A portion of the time had been passed at the Louvre as guest of Louis XIV., who was eight years his junior, but who taught him lessons that were never forgotten. The dissipation, extravagant tastes, and luxurious living at the French court were congenial to the English prince, and it is now our purpose to trace their effects at his home.

Oliver Cromwell died in 1658, and a strong man was needed to take his place. His successor was not able to carry on the government as the Protector had done, and the result was confusion and discord, from which the nation was glad to be relieved by the restoration of the Stuart dynasty in 1660. On the eighth of May of that year, Charles II. was proclaimed king in London. He was at the Hague, but soon set out for England, landing at Dover on the twenty-fifth. It was about noon, the shore was lined with a gallant array of horsemen, citizens, and noblemen ; the mayor came out to receive the king, and presenting him a Bible, his majesty said it was the thing he loved above all things in the world — then he spoke a few words beneath a canopy that was provided for the purpose, and getting into a stately coach, was driven off to Canterbury, amid shouts and expressions of joy, which an eye-witness says were "past imagination."

Men began now to set up "King's Arms," to drink the king's health, and to shout, "God bless King Charles II. !" The simple circumspect Puri tan, with his sober manners and grave dress, is either absent or overlooked, and in his stead we see in the streets, in the drawing-rooms, at church, men wearing brilliant satin doublets, with slashed sleeves, rich point-lace collars, a short cloak carelessly hanging from one shoulder, and a low-crowned Flemish beaver hat, with graceful plumes on their heads. They wore long curling ringlets, that waved about their shoulders, and bore rapiers in their gorgeously embroidered sword-belts. Shame was gone, for the court gave an example of undisguised licentiousness which the people eagerly copied. The theatres were reopened; a new splendor was given the performances; the female characters were personated by women, the scenery was dazzling, the dresses more gay; virtue, truth, and modesty were jeered at; the profligate triumphed, Shakespeare fell into disfavor, and such as Wycherley were honored.

In a word, the Puritan loved piety and Presbyterianism; Charles loved amusement, and agreed to profess Roman Catholicism. The Puritans restrained the people from gay debaucheries; Charles encouraged them. *They* upheld virtue in public and in private; *he* had no shame, and blasphemed all virtue everywhere.

The reaction was complete. Black suits and outward morality gave precedence to ribbons, embroideries, flowing plumes, and loose morals. Literature was no less affected than life, for though Puritans continued to write, as John Bunyan was doing at the moment of the coronation of the restored king, they were not fashionable, nor were their writings popular.

Samuel Butler, 1612–1680, the well-educated son of a yeoman, enjoyed the companionship of John Selden, author of the *Table Talk*, and other advantages which his native brightness led him to improve. He is remembered as the author of *Hudibras*, a burlesque poem of eleven thousand lines, in which he aimed to render ridiculous the habits, manners, customs, and doctrines of the Puritans. It is full of sententious epigrammatic wit, puns, and jokes, often of too broad a character to please a refined taste. Published just after the accession of the new king, it was exceedingly popular with the royalists, and the author rose to a high fame, from which the ephemeral nature of the poem has since served to detract somewhat. Still, Butler is considered the greatest among burlesque writers.

Thomas Otway, 1651–1685, a young writer whose life was full of misery, was the best tragic writer of the period. Among his works are *The Orphan*, and *Venice Preserved*, which are pathetic, intense, eloquent, and sometimes graceful, but on account of the fact that they are disfigured by so much of the fashionable license of the day, they cannot now be performed as they were written.

Sir George Etheridge, 1636–1694, was a comic dramatist of ancient family and excellent education. He is credited with originating the new style of gross immorality, in which, however, he was outstripped by his successors. He wrote *She Would if She Could*, and *The Man of Mode*. Notwithstand ing his elegance, he lived in dissipation and died in a debauch.

JOHN DRYDEN, 1631–1700, the son of an ardent Puritan of ancient family, began his literary life with an *Eulogy on Cromwell*, but soon suddenly forgot his birthright, and welcomed the return of Charles II. The remainder of his life was little more than a series of efforts after literary popularity. Like many professional authors, he wrote a great deal which betokens negligence. With all his defects he is one of the greatest masters of vigorous idiomatic English prose, and of powerful majestic verse. He substituted cold mannerisms for natural language, because tinsel and gilt were more popular than strong sense and solid merit. This foreign disease affected him, and weakened his English heart-power. His earliest and latest efforts were in verse, and in the interval, he produced prose works and plays. Among the latter works are *An Essay on Dramatic Poesy*, *An Essay on Heroic Poetry*, various *Prefaces* and *Dedications*, *Marriage a-la-Mode*, and the *Spanish Friar*. In the first mentioned the author appears as a critic, and has been well characterized as the first one of catholicity of taste and courageous expression. Being marked by the bad as strongly as by the good points of his age, his plays are immoral, but contain many passages of literary merit. Among his poems, besides the eulogies mentioned are, *Annus Mirabilis*, *Absalom and Achitophel*, *Mac-Flecknoe*, *Religio Laici*, *The Hind and Panther*, translations of the *Satires of Juvenal*, and *Persius*, of *Virgil's Georgics* and the *Æneid*, *Fables*, and especially *Alexander's Feast* or *Ode to St. Cecilia.*

SAMUEL PEPYS, 1632–1703, stands almost alone in his peculiar style of writing. Born of an ancient family, but in humble circumstances, he managed to obtain a naval office, which he held under Charles II. and James II., in which he had opportunities not only of improving the fleet, but also of observing all the court intrigues. He recorded in cipher all that he saw, and with a wonderful minuteness. After a century and a half his *Diary* was deciphered and published. It presents in a most vivid and entertaining manner, all the details of dress, amusements, public and private events, and gossip of the day, so that it has the interest of a dramatic novel.

JOHN LOCKE, 1632–1704, imbibed the spirit of liberty and their religious principles from the Puritans. After his graduation at Oxford, he read the works of Francis Bacon, and became a convert from the scholasticism of the Universities to the Baconian system of philosophy. He took a lively interest in public matters, and was very much in the society of the most distinguished politicians and men of letters. His first work in English is the *Essays on the Human Understanding*, the fruit of nearly twenty years of laborious thought, and probably the first attempt in any language at a comprehensive survey of the whole mind and its faculties. It is the work by which the author is best known, and it has exerted a powerful influence upon the course of philosophical inquiry and opinion ever since. Among his other works are, *Letters on Toleration*, *Thoughts concerning Education*, two treatises on *Civil Government*, *The Conduct of the Understanding*, and the *Reasonableness of Christianity*. Locke is described as a man of the most charming personal character, in whom delicacy, forbearance, and true nobility were united with the simplicity of an unpretending scholar, in as near perfection as man has ever exhibited them.

JOHN EVELYN, 1620–1706, was a man of good family who appears to have preserved the purity of his personal character in the midst of the general corruption. His chief works are, *Sylva*, a treatise on forest trees, *Terra*, a work on agriculture and gardening, and his *Diary*, in which he gives a minute and valuable picture of the times.

WILLIAM WYCHERLEY, 1640–1715, the son of royalist parents, was sent to France to be educated, whence he returned a fine gentleman and a papist. After studying a year or two at Oxford, he entered upon a career of *gentlemanly* dissipation, and immoral authorship. His principal plays are, *Love in a Wood*, the *Country Wife*, and the *Plain-Dealer*, all of which reflect the impurity of the writer's personal character, and the superficial polish of the age. He borrowed from the French the plot and morals of some of his works, and it must be added, has wonderfully debased them both. Lord Macaulay's Essay on the *Comic Dramatists of the Restoration* should be read by all who desire to study this period.

GILBERT BURNET, 1643–1715, was bishop of Salisbury, one of our most voluminous writers, and at the same time both active as a politician and eloquent as a preacher. His works are not of the highest merit, but they are valuable for reference as containing many facts not elsewhere found. Among them are, the *History of the Reformation in England*, *Life and Death of the Earl of Rochester*, *History of my Own Times*, *Exposition of the Thirty-nine Articles*, and *Lives of Sir Matthew Hale*, and *Bishop Bedell.* Burnet was a man of rare candor and tolerance. His birth and predilections place him on middle ground between the extremists of the Episcopalians and Presbyterians.

ROBERT SOUTH, 1633–1716, after a course of

brilliant scholarship at Oxford, became one of the most witty, talented, and popular preachers of his day. His *Sermons* are written in an interesting style, and are pithy, pointed, and striking. He is considered to belong to the Arminian school of divines. He often preached before Charles II., and on one occasion used the following language:— "Who that had seen Masaniello, a poor fisherman, with his red cap, and his angle, would have reckoned it possible to see such a pitiful thing, within a week after, shining in his cloth of gold, and with a word or a nod, commanding the whole city of Naples? And who that had beheld such a bankrupt, beggarly fellow as Cromwell, first entering the Parliament House, with a threadbare, torn cloak, greasy hat (perhaps neither of them paid for), could have suspected that, in the space of so few years, he should, by the murder of one King and the banishment of another, ascend the throne?" Though a stanch royalist and an unsparing opponent of Puritanism, Dr. South merits admiration for his noble refusal to accept of preferment, proffered on account of his political and religious principles. He is the subject of many jocose anecdotes, and the sarcastic definition of gratitude, that it is "a sense of obligation for favors expected," is attributed to him.

JOSEPH ADDISON, 1672–1719, exercised a more extensive and beneficial influence on our literature than any man of his day. The style that he formed is still honored, and is more pure, correct, and fascinating than any author had possessed before him. He was educated at Oxford, where he was especially distinguished for his Latin verse, a fact which in connection with his thorough acquaintance with the Latin poets, accounts for the latinity of his style. With regard to the moral service his essays rendered literature and society, Lord Macaulay says in the *Edinburgh Review*, "There still lingered in the public mind a pernicious notion that there was some connection between genius and profligacy, — between the domestic virtues and the sullen formality of the Puritans. That error it is the glory of Addison to have dispelled. He taught the nation that the faith and morality of Hale and Tillotson might be found in company with wit more sparkling than the wit of Congreve, and with humor richer than the humor of Vanbrugh. So effectually indeed did he retort on vice the mockery that had recently been directed against virtue, that since his time the open violation of decency has always been considered among us as the sure mark of a fool. And this revolution, — the greatest and most salutary ever effected by any satirist, — he accomplished, be it remembered, without writing one personal lampoon." We may add that it was on account of the cheerful piety which Addison exemplified in his life, that he could do this. A master of pure eloquence, he was able to paint life and manners, and to use the dangerous weapon of satire in such a way as to effect a social reform. Can we imagine an impulse of this kind coming from any other man of the period? At an early age he began to write poetry, producing, *A Poem to His Majesty*, *Letter from Italy*, and *The Campaign*, written in praise of the Duke of Marlborough, after the victory of Blenheim. His reputation, however, rests principally upon his numerous *Essays* written for the *Tatler*, *Spectator*, and *Guardian*, in which he evinced a brilliancy, humor, taste, and refinement, far in advance of any essayist. Six years before his death his tragedy of *Cato* was put upon the stage. It was received with great applause, and was translated into French, Italian, and German. His latest work, *Evidences of the Christian Religion*, was left unfinished. In some of his *Essays*, Addison incorporated hymns which are marked by a spirit of tender piety and a beauty of diction that have so commended them to the Christian Church, that they are included in the most modern collections of church psalmody. Among these are those beginning, —

> "The spacious firmament on high
> With all the blue, ethereal sky." . . .
>
> "How are thy servants blest, O Lord!"
>
> "When all thy mercies, O my God!" and —
>
> "When rising from the bed of death."

Sir John Vanbrugh, 1666–1726, was of Dutch

ancestry, the son of a rich sugar-baker, and besides being a dramatist, was one of the first architects of his age. He designed the Palace of Blenheim, which government erected for the Duke of Marlborough, and many other buildings. Among his comedies are *The Relapse*, *The Provoked Wife*, *The Provoked Husband*, *Æsop*, and *The Confederacy*. They are crowded with consistent but exaggerated pictures of low life and intrigues. The author became ashamed of what he had written, and in later life planned a new comedy with a virtuous wife as the heroine, but he left the work incomplete; and it was finished by another, with the title of the *Provoked Husband*, as above.

JEREMY COLLIER, 1650–1726, an eminent dissenting divine, was educated at Oxford, and wrote many pamphlets of satirical character, and *Essays* on moral subjects. He is remembered, however, as the author of *A Short View of the Immorality and Profaneness of the English Stage*, which resulted in a discussion of stage morals, continuing for ten years. In this discussion Congreve and Vanbrugh took part. They looked in vain to Dryden for help, but though that author confessed that Collier's strictures were just, he failed to amend. The eyes of the people were opened, however, and a purer taste led very slowly to a purer stage.

SIR ISAAC NEWTON, 1642–1727, the son of a respectable citizen of Lincolnshire, is universally acknowledged to hold the highest rank among natural philosophers of all ages. At the age of twenty-two he discovered the Binomial Theorem; at twenty-three he invented Fluxions; at twenty-four he demonstrated the law of gravitation with regard to the movement of the planets about the sun; and at twenty-seven he revolutionized the study of optics by discovering the non-homogeneity of light, and the differing refrangibility of the rays of which it is composed. His writings belong to the domain of science rather than of literature. They are, *Principia*, *Optics*, *Observations on the Book of Daniel and the Apocalypse*, and *Chronology of the Ancient Kingdoms.*

SIR RICHARD STEELE, 1671–1729, was a wild young man, and of irregular habits throughout life. After getting and losing several fortunes, he died in extreme poverty. In the midst of his youthful dissipations he produced *The Christian Hero*, a moral and religious treatise, embodying the loftiest sentiments of piety and virtue. He was at the time probably intending reformation. The next year he produced a comedy entitled, *The Funeral, or Grief a-la-mode*, which was followed by others, also in contrast to his first work. These were not so successful as the author desired, and in 1709, on the twelfth of April, he began to publish *The Tatler*, a tri-weekly periodical, containing essays and news. In this

Steele was aided by his old schoolfellow Addison, to a limited extent. It was followed by *The Spectator* and *The Guardian*, in both of which Addison was a very important helper. The world owes to Steele's fertile imagination, the characters of *Will Honeycomb*, *Sir Roger de Coverley*, and others of the *Spectator* club. His style was dramatic in its inventions, and he drew his characters with liveliness and facility, but it appears that some of his inventions were much modified and improved by the more refined taste of Addison. At a later period Steele wrote a comedy entitled *The Conscious Lovers*, which is remarkable as being the first one since the Restoration that can be called moral.

William Congreve, 1670–1729, was another of the brilliant but licentious dramatists of the period. He was of good family, thoroughly educated, and as he was well paid for his writings, was free from the usual pecuniary distresses of his contemporaries. He left a large fortune, £10,000; was regarded with great admiration by the poets, and frequented the most learned as well as the most splendid society of his time. In point of immorality his plays are second only to Wycherley. Among his comedies are, *The Old Bachelor*, *The Double Dealer*, *Love for Love*, and *The Way of the World*. Of these *Love for Love* is esteemed his masterpiece. He wrote but one tragedy, which is entitled the *Mourning Bride*.

We began this chapter with a view of Samuel Butler holding the Puritans up to ridicule, which was significant of the change that had come over the spirit of politics and literature. Going from bad to worse, we found Dryden, Etheridge, Vanbrugh, Congreve, and Wycherley in various degree contributing to the debasement of morals and manners. But the evil brought the remedy, and Jeremy Collier only reflected the disgust which had been bred in honest men's minds, when he gave his *Short View* to the world, and opened the purifying discussion that followed its publication.

There were light as well as dark scenes in our view of the era, for did we not see Sir Isaac Newton pushing philosophical and scientific investigation further into the realms of the unseen, than man had ever before looked? Did we not see Joseph Addison, the polished and the pure, proving forever that indecency is folly, and that faith and morality may be the companions of wit and humor?

There is only one more scene to remember, but it was somewhat influential. There were no newspapers worthy of the name in those days, and the centres of information, wit, and criticism were at the *Coffee Houses*, some of which became very celebrated. We have already seen Shakespeare, Jonson, Raleigh, and others at the Mermaid Inn; let us look a moment upon a group we may find in what is known as *Will's*, or the *Wits' Coffee House.* Mr. Pepys says he dropped in, coming home from the

Covent Garden Theatre one night, and heard very witty and pleasant discourse. In a room on the first floor there was a chair by the fireside or at the principal table, for the great literary lion of the day, — the author of the *Hind and the Panther.* Around Dryden were gathered such men as Wycherley, Addison, and others of the wits of the time. There young Pope was brought to see the great poet, and, he says, Dryden was a plump man with a down look, and not very conversable. Another describes him as a decent old man, arbiter of critical disputes. Gathered in little groups about the tables these men ate and drank, snuffed and smoked, gossiped and joked and criticized their songs, epigrams, and satires. The coffee-house was a great London institution, but it is gone now, and men meet more with women, since society has advanced to a higher level.

CHAPTER XI.

MATURE ENGLISH.

Influence of the People, 1700 – 1870.

I. THE AGE OF POPE, 1700 – 1745.

IN our last chapter we saw Steele issuing his *Tatler* three times a week: on Tuesday, Thursday, and Saturday, for the convenience of the post; and we remember the elegant and fashionable papers that he published in it, and which were afterwards continued in the *Spectator*, for the upper and more polished classes of society. A new influence was now exerted upon literature, however, for the people generally were becoming readers. They were stimulated at first by the appeals of Daniel Defoe, and afterwards by the example of the fashionable world. Defoe began his *Review* in 1704, apparently in anticipation of the demand, and continued it until 1712. This was written in the interest of the people, and contained much political discussion. Five years after the *Review* was begun, Steele published the first number of the *Tatler*. The two periodicals differed, as has been shown, in the class of readers for which they were intended, and the influence of the boldness manifested by Defoe in criticizing the government and the court in the name of the people, has never been forgotten in its results. This writer was the son of a non-conformist butcher; was of the people, knew their feelings, sympathized with them; and with copiousness, exuberance, and an inexhaustible power of conception, fought the battles of constitutional liberty, in opposition to the encroachments of the Jacobites. Thus, through Defoe, the people began to exert their influence upon literature as well as upon politics, — an influence which they still refuse to relinquish.

We have already learned that this period may very properly be considered under four divisions. With the first of these the literary life of Alexander Pope corresponds almost to a year. Much has been written on the merits of this poet, and, while there is a wide divergence of opinion regarding his productions, his name is by some classed with those of Chaucer, Spenser, Shakespeare, Milton, and Dryden. His admiration of the latter writer, his predilections for antiquity, and his early study of the classical poets, begat that love of elegance and polish which form marked traits of his poetry. He sought literary excellence as a good in itself, and lost sight of all other aim in writing. The same elegance and polish are prominent characteristics of other writers of the age of Queen Anne, and it has been called, we think erroneously, the Augustan Age of English literature.

Daniel Defoe, 1661–1731, begins the list of writers of the period of the people's influence, and very properly, for he appealed to the people, fought for them, suffered for them, and was gladly heard by them. Belonging to the dissenters, he was excluded from the highest educational advantages, and therefore engaged in mercantile enterprises, but apparently with little success. Entering political life as an Independent, he wrote tracts and pamphlets almost without number. Among these the *True-born Englishman* became immediately popular. In 1702, he wrote the *Shortest Way with Dissenters*, in which, in the character of a high churchman, he ironically proposed hanging the ministers and banishing the people who did not conform to the religion of government. His political efforts brought him to the pillory and prison. Upon his liberation he determined to write moral and religious works, and in pursuance of this resolution, published the *Family Instructor*, and *Religious Courtship*. In 1719, at the age of fifty-eight, he began a career of fictitious authorship, which has carried his name down to posterity. Among his writings of this class are, the *Life and Surprising Adventures of Robinson Crusoe*, *Life and Piracies of Captain Singleton*, *Journal of the Plague in* 1665, *Memoirs of a Cavalier*, and the *Political History of the Devil.* Resembling Bunyan in his unlimited command of plain, straightforward English, and being able to throw a remarkable air of reality into his fiction, he creates a wonderful sympathy between his heroes and the reader. His *Memoir of a Cavalier* and *Journal of the Plague* were thus both of them accepted by intelligent men as narratives of fact. In addition to a vast number of other works, Defoe published his tri-weekly *Review*, which exhibited force and vigor. The moral teachings of his writings are generally unexceptionable.

JOHN GAY, 1688–1732, was an amiable and popular poet who wrote in the spirit of the former age of dependence upon the great. At the age of twenty-six he produced *The Shepherd's Week*, which was followed by *Trivia, or the Art of Walking the Streets of London*, and other pieces. His fame rests, however, upon his *Fables*, his ballad of *Black-Eyed Susan*, and the *Beggar's Opera*. The last, though of exceptionable morality, was very successful, and the author was well paid for his labors. Gay spent his later years as a member of the household of the Duke of Queensberry, where, as Thackeray says, "he was lapped in cotton, and had his plate of chicken, and his saucer of cream, and frisked, and barked, and wheezed, and grew fat, and so ended." He was buried in Westminster Abbey.

ALEXANDER POPE, 1688–1744, the most brilliant writer of this period, who has been called the "prince of the artificial school of English poetry," was the delicate son of a wealthy retired merchant, who lived on the borders of Windsor Forest. Pope was of irregular education, was fond of fashionable society, an admirer of Dryden, a protégé of Wycherley, and the friend of many a worthier man of note. His poems exhibit ease, grace, terseness, wit, beauty of versification, and good taste, but they are deficient in genius, sublimity, catholicity, and other traits of the true poet. His intimacy with Lord Bolingbroke, who was a skeptic and libertine, is apparent in its bad influence upon some of Pope's works, but is especially manifest in his *Essay on Man*, otherwise one of the best of his efforts. Among his other works are, *Ode to Solitude*, written at nine years of age, *Essay on Criticism*, *Rape of the Lock*, *Translation of the Iliad of Homer*, and the *Dunciad.*

JONATHAN SWIFT, 1667–1745, was an intellectual giant whose genius was clouded by mysterious circumstances that have never been explained. He was a morbidly sensitive youth, and his life, passed amid the conflicts of improper love-passions, ended in the gloom of insanity, which had probably been smouldering in his nature through many years of his enigmatical life. Through the influence of the Tory party, to which he belonged, he became Dean of St. Patrick's Cathedral, Dublin, but he had little religious feeling. His works, though models of idiomatic English, forcible satire, keen humor, and vigorous imagination, are in parts so marked by his infidelity, malignity, and filthiness as to be of pernicious tendency. His principal works are, *Political Pamphlets*, *Tale of a Tub*, *Gulliver's Travels*, and *An Argument showing the Inconvenience of Abolishing Christianity.*

JAMES THOMSON, 1700–1748, was a graceful poet of romantic tastes and lazy habits. His attention was turned from divinity to poetry, when at the University of Edinburgh, by a suggestion of the professor of divinity, who told Thomson that if he intended to become a minister he must keep a stricter rein over his imagination. He had the faculty of looking at common things in a poetic manner, and versified with purity of diction and harmony of rhythm. He was one of the first Scotchmen who attained eminence as writers of English poetry. Thomson's *Seasons* contain many charming descriptions of nature, of which he was exceedingly fond. *The Castle of Indolence* is another composition in verse, written in the beautiful style of Spenser's *Faery Queen*, and exhibiting the traits of Thomson's character and life. Among his other productions is an ambitious poem entitled *Liberty*, which he considered his masterpiece, but it has never been popular.

ISAAC WATTS, 1674–1748, was the precocious son of a pious teacher of Southampton. After a thorough education, begun at home, and finished at various good schools, he became a dissenting preacher. In consequence of the failure of his health, he became the guest of Sir Thomas Abney, at whose house he was entertained for thirty-six years. With no cares to disturb him, Dr. Watts pursued his studies, and produced his *Hymns* of various degrees of literary merit, but of a singularly pure Christian tone; his *Logic* and his *Improvement of the Mind*, upon which his wide reputation firmly rests. The sacred poetry of Dr. Watts has so firm hold upon the affections of Christians everywhere, that no collection of psalms or hymns is considered complete without a large number of those composed by him. A late judicious writer observes, "The period of English hymnology ushered in by Watts, continued by Doddridge and the Wesleys, is in some respects more marked than any in the history of Christian song. . . . . Up to his time nothing but versions of the Psalms — the standard of perfection, in which was, *first*, literal and prosaic adherence to the original, and *secondly*, rhyme or its caricature — had any acknowledged right to a place in worship. . . . . He asserted the right of a *Christian hymn*, founded on *any* portion of inspired truth, to take its place in the service of song. The ancient Church had acknowledged it; the churches of the Reformation had acknowledged it. Watts gained the right for *his* psalms and hymns, and so for all, by writing such as were so superior that they compelled the recognition. . . . . He unloosed the spirit of Christian song, which soared aloft and has been brooding over choice souls, ever since. To Dr. Watts we are indebted for Doddridge, Toplady, the Wesleys, Cowper, Newton, Anne Steele, Bishop Heber, Lyte, Montgomery. He created the hymnology to which they made such rich additions." Apart, however, from his labors in this direction, Dr. Watts exercised a powerful influence in the formation of public opinion, and his writings have contributed much to keep alive the spirit of freedom, toleration, and piety wherever the English language is spoken.

LORD BOLINGBROKE, 1678–1751, was a friend of Pope and Swift, a man of elegance of manners, of dissipated early life, of political intrigues, and of deistical principles, but as a writer possessing a stately and flowing style, full of words and finish, but deficient in accuracy, depth, and heartiness. Political considerations forced him into a voluntary banishment to France, where he produced the greater part of his writings. Among them are, *Reflections on Exile*, *Letters on the Study of History*, and *Letter on the True Use of Retirement.* Upon his return he wrote *The Idea of a Patriot King.* Bolingbroke is now little read, another proof that infidel writers seldom enjoy long-continued popularity.

BISHOP BERKELEY, 1684–1753, was an enthusiastic, romantic, and pure-minded philosopher, who united philanthropy and learning to the finest traits of the Irish character. He was a native of Kilkenny County, Ireland, and rose to be Bishop of Cloyne, in which office he died. He was a man of great genius, but of Utopian schemes. He argued that all sensible qualities, such as hardness, figure, etc., are mere ideas without material existence. His Christian benevolence led him to form a purpose to convert the American savages to Christianity, but his plans failed, though he spent five years in this country. He became a patron of Yale College, then in its infancy, and took a deep interest in Columbia College, New York. Being fully convinced of the future greatness of America, he wrote the prophetic and almost proverbial lines in which occur the words, —

> "Westward the course of empire takes its way!"

Berkeley was a friend of Pope, Steele, Swift, and the other wits of the day, who, while they loved him, and admired his purity and enthusiasm, laughed at his benevolent vagaries. His chief works are, *The Theory of Vision*, *Principles of Human Knowledge*, and *The Minute Philosopher*.

Henry Fielding, 1707–1754, was a writer of noble birth, good education, and dissipated habits, who having become a London police magistrate, composed novels in which he depicted low life as it then existed. Being full of indelicacy, his works though powerful and extraordinary, cannot be read in the family circle, and are not popular at the present day. Among his writings are, *Plays*, *Joseph Andrews*, *Tom Jones*, *Amelia*, and *Jonathan Wild.* He has been called the father of the English novel, by some who consider that Richardson did not escape the trammels of the French romance.

William Collins, 1720–1756, was of humble origin, but had good educational advantages. His life, full of disappointment, dissipation, and unfulfilled projects, ended in insanity. He died at an early age, after producing some of the finest lyrics in our language. He was the author of *Ode to Evening*, *The Passions*, *Ode on the Superstitions of the Highlands*, *The Dirge in Cymbeline*, and other pieces.

Samuel Richardson, 1689–1761, the son of a cabinet-maker, and of indifferent education, was brought up as a printer, and became the originator of the novel of high life. In youth he was noted for his facility in story-telling, and was a favorite of the young girls, for three of whom he wrote their love-letters. These circumstances exercised a strong influence, and induced him, at the age of fifty, to write his first novel, *Pamela, or Virtue Rewarded*, in the epistolary style. Though comprised in four large volumes, this was eagerly read and highly praised. It was followed, in 1749, by the history of *Clarissa Harlowe*, in eight volumes. In 1753 Richardson published *Sir Charles Grandison*, also in the form of letters, and in seven volumes. These were marked by minute and tedious descriptions which, in our age, would cause them to be scarcely read at all. Sir Walter Scott says, "It requires a reader to be in some degree acquainted with the huge folios of inanity over which our ancestors yawned themselves to sleep, ere he can estimate the delight they must have experienced from this unexpected return to truth and nature." Richardson's novels are pictures of the heart, minute and truthful, and in this lay their power, and the reason for their popularity.

Allan Ramsay, 1685–1758, was the son of a Scotch miner. His early advantages of education were limited. He was apprenticed to a wig-maker at the age of fifteen, but after marriage opened a book-seller's shop, and also produced much poetry of varied style as well as degrees of merit. His masterpiece is the *Gentle Shepherd*, a pastoral drama, in which Scotch country life is depicted in all its natural simplicity. By some critics this is considered the finest idyllic drama in the world. In the title the word *gentle* signifies well-born or noble, a meaning inhering in the word gentleman. Being in the northern dialect, the *Gentle Shepherd* was very popular in Scotland, but notwithstanding its provincial language, it was republished both in London and Dublin. Ramsay wrote many popular lyrics, among which the *Yellow-haired Laddie*, and *Lochaber no More* are still dear to the hearts of his countrymen.

LADY MONTAGUE, 1690–1762, whose family name was Pierrepoint, was the daughter of the Duke of Kingston, was highly educated, became the pet of the wits of the reign of Queen Anne, and at the age of twenty-two married Edward Wortley Montague. During two years of the ten that she lived with her husband, he was English ambassador at Constantinople. Her literary fame rests upon her *Letters*, published after her death. Epistolary composition was much cultivated at this period by Walpole, Cowper, Pope, and other men who stood high in literary circles, but Lady Montague excels them all in vivacity, sarcasm, ease, elegance, and the other traits that distinguish letters from essays. She challenges comparison with Madame de Sévigné, the great letter-writer of the time of Louis XIV., who alone is to be mentioned as her equal. In the letters of the French lady there is a delicate motherly affection that is entirely wanting in the English writer. While Lady Montague is deficient in delicacy of taste, as well as in other gentle traits, she is superior to Madame de Sévigné in intellectual culture. One is gossipy and brilliant, the other vivacious, observing, philosophical.

LAURENCE STERNE, 1713–1768, was a graduate of Cambridge University, and an eccentric and inconsistent clergyman of the Church of England. His reputation as an author was established upon the publication of *Tristram Shandy*, an odd, and somewhat immoral novel, with little plot, and consisting chiefly of slightly connected sketches of humor and fancy. In 1768 *The Sentimental Journey* appeared. It contains, among many gems of thought and sentiment, a great deal that is impure and profane.

TOBIAS GEORGE SMOLLETT, 1721–1771, was of a good family, his grandfather being a member of the Scottish parliament. He manifested, at a very early age, a tendency to ridicule by his abundant satirical verses on his school-fellows. He was educated for the medical profession, but the passion for miscellaneous reading, which often besets men of genius, diverted his attention from the proper direction of his energies. His principal novels are *Roderick Random*, *Peregrine Pickle*, and *Humphry Clinker*, the last of which breathes a kindlier spirit, and is livelier than the other two. Smollett spent much of his life away from his native country, where he was cordially entertained, and was the recipient of flattering attentions from the literati. His novels are original and amusing, the characters being numerous, but of very different values as representations of life. He appears to nave had no moral purpose, and in this respect is much inferior to Richardson, while like other writers of the period, he disfigured his pages with much that is coarse and disgusting. Smollett is also known as the author of *A Complete History of England to the Peace of Aix-la-Chapelle*, written with fluency and fairness. A portion of it is usually printed as a continuation of Hume's history.

Our view of this period of literature will not be complete until we depict another character that is often referred to by the writers of the time.

Nor far from Bunhill-Fields, where Bunyan, Watts, Owen, Blake, and many other celebrities are interred, is a part of the city of London that is peculiar even there by reason of its filthy and labyrinthine courts, its antique houses, and its depressing air of poverty. It and its denizens are mentioned by Pope in his *Dunciad* in these words: —

> "Not with less glory mighty Dulness crowned,
> Shall take through *Grub Street* her triumphant round·
> And, her Parnassus glancing o'er at once,
> Behold a hundred sons, and each a dunce."

In Grub Street dwelt those who wrote ballads, and did hack work for the book-sellers. Their poverty-stricken character is described in an imaginary account written by Pope and his friends.

"At a tallow chandler's in Petty-France, half-way under the blind arch, ask for the historian, at the *Bedstead and Bolster*, a music house in Moorfields, two translators in bed together; at a blacksmith's shop in the Friars, a Pindaric writer in red stockings; at Mr. Summer's, a thief-catcher's in Lewkner's Lane, the man that wrote against the impiety of Mr. Rowe's plays," etc.

The low nature of these performances has fixed the name of *Grub Street* upon "bad matter expressed in a bad manner, false confused histories, low creeping poetry, and grovelling prose," whether written in that locality or elsewhere.

We have generally looked upon the other aspect of author life in this chapter, but we must remember that, as the proverb tells us, "a medal always has two sides." In this era authors were very successful or very miserable, and we can see very little of any intermediate condition. The poor hack writers wrote prefaces, prologues, indexes, reviews, almanacs, in short anything, receiving, as Macaulay says, the wages of a ditcher. Some of these, like Johnson, struggled manfully through their trials, and rose to fame, but they were few; the far greater number perished prematurely, worn out by the toils of the way, or destroyed by their own dissipations.

As we look over the Age of Pope, we see that we have made progress. On our increasing list of good books we have recorded the titles of many that will never be wiped out. Among these are,

Robinson Crusoe, *Rape of the Lock*, the *Dunciad*, *Gulliver's Travels*, Thomson's *Seasons*, Watts's *Hymns*, *Improvement of the Mind*, and *Logic*, Collins's *Odes*, Richardson's *Pamela*, Ramsay's *Drama* and *Lyrics*, Lady Montague's *Letters*, and others.

CHAPTER XII.

MATURE ENGLISH.

Influence of the People, 1700–1870.

II. THE AGE OF JOHNSON, 1745–1800

HE second division of the period of the people's influence extends from 1745 to the end of the century. During these years the figure that had the greatest prominence was that of Samuel Johnson, the author of that great national work, the *Dictionary of the English Language*. Lord Macaulay calls Johnson "the last survivor of a genuine race of Grub Street hacks," and in closing an article on the subject in the *Edinburgh Review*, the same eminent writer presents us the following picture of the room of the *Literary Club* of which Dr. Johnson was a member: —

"The club-room is before us, and the table on which stand the omelet for Nugent, and the lemons for Johnson. There are the spectacles of Burke, and the tall thin form of Langton; the courtly sneer of Beauclerk, and the beaming smile of Garrick; Gibbon tapping his snuff-box, and Sir Joshua with his trumpet in his ear. In the foreground is that strange figure which is as familiar to us as the figures of those among whom we have been brought up, — the gigantic body, the huge massy face, seamed with the scars of disease; the brown coat, the black worsted stockings, the gray wig with a scorched foretop; the dirty hands, the nails bitten and pared to the quick. We see the eyes and mouth moving with convulsive twitches; we see the heavy form rolling; we hear it puffing; and then comes the 'Why sir!' and the 'What then, sir?' the 'No sir!' and the 'You don't see your way through the question, sir!'

"What a singular destiny has been that of this remarkable man! To be regarded in his own age as a classic, and in ours as a companion; to have received from his contemporaries that full homage which men of genius have in general received only from posterity; to be more intimately known to posterity than other men are known to their contemporaries! That kind of fame which is commonly the most transient, is in his case the most durable. The reputation of those writings which he probably expected to be immortal, is every day fading; while those peculiarities of manner, and that careless table-talk, the memory of which he probably thought would die with him, are likely to be remembered as long as the English language is spoken in any quarter of the globe."

Such was Dr. Johnson, the most influential author of his day, who raised himself to his post of supremacy in the face of obstacles which would have deterred a less energetic character from making even an attempt. His own earnestness and profundity influenced many who surrounded him. The peculiarity of his diction was more easily imitated by weaker minds, than his deep sense, and the style of language called Johnsonese, with little to recommend it, obtained a temporary prevalence. It was Dr. Johnson's inability to write in plain short words, at which his friend Goldsmith aimed when he very wittily said, "If you were to write a fable about little fishes, doctor, you would make the little fishes talk like whales."

Literature in our own country was at this time very strongly marked by the earnestness and strength with which religious and political discussions are generally characterized. American literature may be considered in three periods. I. *The Colonial Period,* extending from 1620 to 1775. II. *The Revolutionary Period,* from 1775 to 1830. III. *The American Period,* from 1830 to the present time.

During the Colonial period the great subjects of discussion were connected with religion. Among the writers of the era were Increase and Cotton Mather, Charles Chauncey, Samuel Johnson, of Columbia College, Mather Byles, Ezra Stiles, of Yale College, Benjamin Franklin, John Bartram, Thomas Prince, Thomas Hutchinson, and Jonathan Edwards. The last writer is styled by Sir James Mackintosh *the* metaphysician of America, of whose power of subtle argument the same high authority asserts that it is "perhaps unmatched, certainly unsurpassed among men." According to Robert Hall, Edwards was the first in any country or age.

The Revolutionary period is marked by no less earnestness, though the topics discussed were of a political character. Among the literary men of this time were, James Otis, Josiah Quincy, Jr., Timothy Pickering, George Washington, Alexander Hamilton, John Jay, James Madison, John Adams, Fisher Ames, Jeremy Belknap, Chief Justice Marshall, William Wirt, Alexander Graydon, Samuel Hopkins, Timothy Dwight, Joseph Bellamy, Noah Worcester, David Rittenhouse, Lindley Murray, Philip Frenau, John Trumbull, Joel Barlow, Joseph Hopkinson, Joseph Dennie, and Thomas Jefferson. The last named was the author of the *Declaration of Independence*, in which the concise, direct, forcible, dignified, and eloquent traits of the authorship of the period appear to have culminated. The Revolutionary period, then, was marked by eloquent discussions of legal and constitutional principles.

The last period of American literature will be referred to in Chapters XIII. and XIV.

JONATHAN EDWARDS, 1703–1758, was the only son of a highly educated Connecticut clergyman. He was precocious in the development of the reasoning powers, full of imagination and enthusiasm, and of remarkable habits of observation and reflection. After graduation at Yale College, he studied theology for two years, and before he was nineteen years of age was settled over a Calvinistic church in New York city. His subsequent life was spent as tutor in Yale College, pastor at Northampton, Massachusetts, missionary to the Indians at Stockbridge, and as president of the college at Princeton, New Jersey, where he died a few weeks after his inauguration. He was one of the most profound thinkers the world has ever seen, and studied out in his quiet places of retirement those remarkable metaphysical schemes which have exerted a world-wide influence. As a metaphysician, Dr. Chalmers ranks him above all his contemporaries, and Dugald Stewart says he does not yield in logical acuteness to any disputant bred in the universities of Europe. His chief works are, *Freedom of the Will*, *History of Redemption*, *True Virtue*, and *Original Sin*.

THOMAS GRAY, 1716–1771, the son of a money-broker of London, became, after a course of study at Eton and Cambridge, and a tour through France and Italy, the greatest of the purely lyric poets of England. He lived very quietly at Cambridge, enjoying his studies of the classics, of antiquity, and of nature. There he cultivated the fashionable epistolary composition, in which he excelled, and there he produced the lyrics which have given him fame as a man of deep learning, careful observation, quiet humor, strong sympathy, tenderness, fancy, and exquisitely refined taste. He is best known by his *Elegy written in a Country Church-yard*, which is often reprinted in our day. Among his other works are, *The Progress of Poesy*, *The Bard*, *Ode to Spring*, *Hymn to Adversity*, *On a Distant Prospect of Eton*, and *Letters*, all of which display the graces of taste and scholarship for which he was remarkable.

Oliver Goldsmith, 1728–1774, was the son of the Protestant rector of Pallas, Ireland. He was sent to various schools, and to Trinity College, Dublin, but was never a superior scholar. Of gentle heart, and unable to grapple successfully with real life, he at first gained a precarious subsistence by writing and selling street ballads. For a year he travelled through Flanders, France, Germany, Switzerland, and Italy, trudging often all day on foot, and playing merry tunes on his flute for his supper and bed. A part of this year he was companion of a rich young man who needed a guide; and in Italy he won some money and food by disputing in a university with the doctors. The fruit of this trip was apparent in *The Traveller* and in the picture of the *Philosophic Vagabond*, in the *Vicar of Wakefield*. In 1757 he wrote his *Chinese Letters*, for the periodicals, and also the *Life of Beau Nash*, and the *History of England*. He afterwards produced the comedies of *The Good Natured Man*, and *She Stoops to Conquer.* These were followed by the *History of Rome*, the *History of Greece*, the *History of Animated Nature*, and by the poem of the *Deserted Village.* The grace, ease, elegance, delicacy, and purity of these writings caused the author's society to be courted by the most admired wits, authors, and statesmen of the day, in whose company we saw him at the Literary Club mentioned in the beginning of this chapter. His life was made miserable by his weakness of purpose, prodigality, and bad habits; and his large income, sometimes as great as $9,000 a year, did not prove sufficient to keep him from leaving heavy debts unpaid at his death.

DAVID HUME, 1711–1776, one of the most distinguished Scotchmen of any era, was a metaphysician and a historian. He was born in Edinburgh, the second son of an old family; he was bred to the law, which he disliked, and after a variety of changes gave himself wholly to literature. His first writings, *A Treatise of Human Nature*, and *Moral and Philosophical Essays*, were only tolerably successful. He next wrote *Political Discourses*, and *Inquiry concerning the Principles of Morals.* In 1754, he produced the first volume of the *History of England*, on which his fame rests, of which but forty-five copies were sold the first year. Deeply chagrined, the author meditated a change of name and flight from home. The tide turned in his favor, however, and in 1762 he had completed his fourth volume in triumph. Picturesque, dramatic, and beautiful, his works are still read, though they contain errors of fact occasioned by his lack of diligence and research, and errors of doctrine, caused by his skeptical religious philosophy. Doubting almost everything, he is untrustworthy, and often a false guide, and must rank second to the conscientious and careful students who have succeeded him.

SAMUEL JOHNSON, 1709–1784, from whom this period takes its name, was the son of a humble bookseller of Lichfield. The premature death of his father left him without the means of obtaining a complete education, and, after unsuccessful attempts at gaining a livelihood in other ways, he went to London, where for some years he was a bookseller's drudge. His pen was continually at work writing pamphlets, prefaces, epitaphs, essays, and biographical memoirs, many of which were published in the *Gentleman's Magazine.* His poem *London*, published in 1738, laid the foundation of his fame. The next year it was followed by the *Vanity of Human Wishes*, in imitation of one of the Satires of Juvenal. His chief prose works are, *The Rambler*, *The Idler*, *Rasselas Prince of Abyssinia*, *Lives of the Poets*, *Journey to the Hebrides*, and the *Dictionary of the English Language.* The last was the product of vast labor, and occupied the author eight years. It is deserving of very high praise, though necessarily defective in many particulars. The illustrative quotations are so interesting that few open the volume for reference without reading much more than the passage they looked for. The author's style is marked by the recurrence of stately words of Latin origin, by measured phrase, and by a lack of simplicity. Though the style of Johnson may be admired in his own works, it was rendered ridiculous through the extravagance of his imitators. His life is familiar to the world through the inimitable record made by his friend and obsequious companion James Boswell.

Benjamin Franklin, 1706–1790, the son of a tallow-chandler of Boston, Massachusetts, began life as a journeyman printer, hoping to obtain thereby the advantages of education. By the diligent use of his spare time, he improved his mind and style of writing. He afterwards pursued his vocation in Philadelphia, and in London. In 1729 he became publisher of the *Pennsylvania Gazette*, and engaged in bookselling. In 1732 he began to publish *Poor Richard's Almanac*, which was successfully continued for nearly a quarter-century. In 1736 he entered political life, and was thenceforth a prominent champion of the Colonies. He was at different times Postmaster-general, Minister to France, Governor of Pennsylvania, one of the framers of the Federal Constitution, and in short, as Bancroft says, "the greatest diplomatist of the eighteenth century." He wrote *Scientific Papers*, *The Way to Wealth*, *Letters*, and an *Autobiography*, which last has lately been republished by the Hon. John Bigelow, late United States Minister in France. Dr. Franklin's style is homely, practical, and pointed.

Adam Smith, 1723–1790, was a Scotchman, well educated, first at Glasgow University, and afterwards at Oxford, who, adopting the pursuit of letters, became professor at Glasgow, and as the result of persistent study, produced in 1759 his *Theory of the Moral Sentiments*, and in 1776, his greater work, *An Inquiry into the Nature and Causes of the Wealth of Nations*. The first of these is an eloquent philosophical discussion, and the second is the work which laid the foundation of the modern science of political economy.

William Robertson, 1721–1793, was another Scotchman, who until 1759, was only known as an eloquent Presbyterian preacher. In that year he produced his *History of Scotland during the Reigns of Queen Mary, and of King James VI., till his Accession to the Crown of England.* This judicious work gave the author a renown as immediate and well founded as it was surprising to his contemporaries. Ten years later his *History of the Reign of Charles V.* being equally well received, he derived a competence from his publications. In 1777 he produced his *History of America*, a work containing parts that are of almost poetic interest. In 1791 he appeared the last time as an author with his *Historical Disquisition concerning the Knowledge which the Ancients had of India*, a work of merit, but which was based on sources of information that were not always trustworthy.

EDWARD GIBBON, 1737–1794, was a delicate youth of gentle birth, and a diligent student almost from infancy. His education was thorough, having been pursued both in England and on the Continent. In religious views he experienced various changes until he became a deist, a fact which must be considered while reading his works. His studies were pursued in the fields of history with wonderful care and great discrimination. He says that while he sat musing amidst the ruins of the Capitol in Rome, on the fifteenth of October, 1764, while the barefooted friars were singing vespers in the temple of Jupiter, the idea of writing the decline and fall of that city first started to his mind. Twenty-three years later he laid down his pen in his summerhouse at Lausanne, Switzerland, having completed the greatest historical work in the language. The title is the *Decline and Fall of the Roman Empire*, and the history begins with the reign of Trajan, A. D. 98, and closes with the capture of Constantinople by the Turks in 1453. It has been said that everything except Christianity is embellished by Gibbon's pen. Lord Byron wrote of him that he —

> ". . . . Shaped his weapon with an edge severe,
> Sapping a solemn creed with solemn sneer;"

lines which show Byron's estimate of the attitude which Gibbon assumed toward the Christian faith. His style is pompous, ornate, and lacking generous enthusiasm. While we give him all the literary credit he deserves, it may well be added that the highest productions of literature have never been the fruit of infidelity; the clearest, strongest, and most bracing thought having always been closely allied to a strong faith in the revelations of Scripture. Gibbon was a member of Parliament during eight sessions at the time of our Revolutionary War, and supported Lord North in his efforts to coerce the Americans.

ROBERT BURNS, 1759–1796, called the Shakespeare of Scotland, was a man of slight education, — but it was the education of the heart, based upon the Bible, — who owed his general knowledge to the *Spectator*, the works of Pope and Ramsay, and the ballads of his country. Burns first appeared as a poet in 1786, and immediately attained an influence and popularity greater than any other Scottish poet has reached. Like Cowper in England, he worked to bring poetry back to truth and nature. His convivial habits proved his ruin. In spite of his many good traits of mind and heart, Burns presents in his life a mournful exhibition of admirable simplicity and manly genius, rising to charm the world, only to be lost in the drunkard's early grave

When yet a plowman, he wrote lines to a *Mountain Daisy*, and the *Mousie's Nest*, which are full of tender beauty. His love poems are well known. Among them *Ae Fond Kiss and then We Sever*, is celebrated. His *Scots wha hae wi Wallace bled*, is a powerful patriotic lyric; the *Cotter's Saturday Night* is a lovely picture of domestic religion, in which the poet's father and the old family Bible are interesting features. *Tam O'Shanter* is a weird tale of a market-day carousal, a midnight ride, a witch dance in the Alloway kirk, with other incidents; and his other poems possess the same traits which endear them to the Scottish heart, notwithstanding some coarseness and occasional flings at religion, the purity of which necessarily condemned his private life.

EDMUND BURKE, 1730–1797, holds the first place among the orators and political writers of England. A native of Dublin, he inherited many good Irish traits, and spent many of his early days in the county of Cork, not far from the river Mulla, and the ruins of Castle Kilcolman, where in the days of Elizabeth, Edmund Spenser lived and wrote. At the age of twenty Burke went to London, and began to write for his daily bread, his first productions being *A Vindication of Natural Society*, *The Sublime and Beautiful*, an *American History*, in two volumes, and *The Annual Register*, published by Dodsley. These brought the young author to the notice of Dr. Johnson and the other eminent men of the day. In 1766 he entered Parliament, and became prominent as an opponent of the American war, a subject that furnished the theme of many of his most eloquent efforts. In 1788 he delivered his grandest speech, on the occasion of the *Impeachment of Warren Hastings*, Governor-general of India. In 1790 he warned England against the dangers that were threatening France, in his *Reflections on the French Revolution*. In this occurs the spirited account of Marie Antoinette, and the age of chivalry, found in many of our text-books. Burke's last works were, *Letters on a Regicide Peace*, *Letter to a Noble Lord*, and *Observations on the Conduct of the Minority*.

William Cowper, 1731–1800, one of the most delicate, free, and idiomatic of English poets, was unfortunately the victim of religious melancholy which deepened into insanity. From this state of mind he had several recoveries. Between 1776 and 1794, Cowper was only deranged for six months, and it was during this period that his principal works were produced. These are, *The Task*, *Hymns*, *Translation of Homer*, *John Gilpin*, and *Lines to my Mother's Picture*. Possessed of an elevated genius, and of a desire to make mankind better by writing, Cowper's poetry is of a healthy tone, is unaffected and highly esteemed. The wit exhibited n the writings of many of those whose unregulated lives we have been considering, is much of it lost to the world on account of the offensive setting, in which a debased taste displayed it, but the simple faith of Cowper lives in his hymns, and will always exert a powerful influence. Southey calls Cowper the best of English letter-writers, which is high praise, but not undeserved. His hymns are among the best and most frequently used of any in the language.

TIMOTHY DWIGHT, 1752–1817, a native of Northampton and a grandson of Jonathan Edwards, was thoroughly educated, and became in 1795 president of Yale College, in which he had been a student. Among his principal writings are, *The History, Eloquence, and Poetry of the Bible*, *Greenfield Hill*, a poem in seven parts; a version of *Watts's Psalms*, *Travels in New England and New York*, and *Theology Explained and Defended in a Series of Sermons*, in five volumes. These are full of sentiments of religion and patriotism. The last mentioned, his *System of Theology*, is a standard work in America and England, and upon it his reputation as an author mainly depends. His reputation as president of Yale College has caused his memory to be revered by many who came under his influence there, and by all who are interested in the prosperity of that important institution. Dr. Dwight's popularity with the students was unbounded, and he introduced reforms in the college management which have had a permanent influence.

Our book-shelves are filling up. The period just considered has given us Dr. Johnson's wonderful *Dictionary*, and by its side stand the volumes of his *Rambler* and *Idler*, with their weighty essays, while not far off is the book he wrote to pay his mother's funeral expenses, — *Rasselas, Prince of Abyssinia.* On another shelf we read the names of Hume and Gibbon, and Robertson on our new but substantial histories. There too are Burke's complete works, and Franklin's, and Smith's *Wealth of Nations*, and Edwards on the *Will*, and on *Original Sin*, which were worked out under the elms at Stockbridge. Another shelf shows us Cowper's *Task*, Goldsmith's *Vicar of Wakefield*, and *Deserted Village*, and Gray's *Elegy written in a Country Church-yard.* Surely the age of Johnson has not left us without marks of its earnestness and depth, if it does include the sweet lyrics of Burns and Gray, and the descriptive verse of Cowper and Goldsmith !

CHAPTER XIII.

MATURE ENGLISH.

Influence of the People, 1700–1870.

III. AGE OF POETICAL ROMANCE, 1800–1830.

N the period we have just considered, there was a notable change in the poetry of our literature. Pope and Dryden had passed away, and their successors, Goldsmith, Cowper, and Gray, had turned from classical subjects to more romantic themes.

Let us pause for a moment to consider the influences that effected this result.

A complete investigation of the subject would lead us to a very interesting discussion of the international relations of literature, for the same change, in its essential traits, has been noticed also in both Germany and France. In the latter country it has been ascribed to German and English influence, and the change in England has been attributed to the influence of France and Germany.

In Germany a national literature was rapidly developing, and on the lists of authors and thinkers there we find the names of Lessing, Bürger, Wieland, Klopstock, Goethe, Schiller, Kant, Fichte, and Jacobi.

In France, during the Reign of Terror, from the destruction of the Bastile in 1789 to the execution of Robespierre in 1794, and the Italian campaign of Napoleon in 1796, while the nation was convulsed in a blind struggle after liberty, a romantic school was inaugurated in literature.

It is certain that in each of the three nations mentioned there was a spontaneous and simultaneous forsaking of the classical for the romantic style, not only among poets, but also among prose writers.

The diffusion of knowledge, the progress of republican ideas, and the more liberal views held both by the scholar and the churchman, had already begun to impress the age; and the lighter literature which has since been so remarkably developed, was well adapted to furnish relief and recreation in the more intense life of modern times.

We are now prepared to consider those writers, who, after Dr. Johnson and his friends had left the stage, introduced, and for a generation continued to produce, what now constitutes our treasures of poetical romance.

The period was one of intense conflicts, of much passionate emotion, and the expression of writers was to so great an extent found in song, that no era presents us such an array of poets.

In 1765, Thomas Percy, a bishop of the English Established Church, gave a powerful impetus to this tendency by the publication of his *Reliques of English Poetry*, which consisted of heroic ballads, songs, and metrical tales connected with early English literature, accompanied by a dissertation on our ancient bards and minstrelsy.

In 1796, Sir Walter Scott began his brilliant career by publishing a translation of Bürger's *Lenore*, which was followed by his other stirring poems. The rising splendor of Lord Byron turned Scott's pen from poetry to the field of prose romance, in which he had no dangerous competitor.

In 1798, William Wordsworth and his sister took up their abode among the charming lakes and mountains which render the counties of Cumberland and Westmoreland so attractive to tourists. In 1800, Wordsworth published a new edition of a volume of his *Ballads* that had previously been neglected. His endeavor was to turn the public taste from pomposity to simplicity, from a devotion to antiquity to the love of nature and humanity. In these efforts he was supported by Southey, Coleridge, De Quincey, Wilson, and others, to whom the sobriquet *Lake School* was applied, as if they had founded a poetical sect upon a new theory of composition. As we consider the authors generally included in this school, we shall find that though they sympathized in many points, there were also important differences in their style and sentiments.

Soon after the opening of the present century, the writers of America began to exhibit tokens of increased capacity and greater cultivation, and to develop a national literature. The present generation has seen the shackles of imitation drop off one by one, and the freedom of originality is growing more marked. Thus, in moral and political science, in law, in fiction, and history, in oratory, in humorous, sentimental, and thoughtful writings, the range of American thought has been vast, and our authors have been acknowledged by the constant reproduction of their works in all civilized countries. The increasing number of good writers in the United States as well as in Great Britain, will make it necessary to exclude from our notice many who in a larger work would demand no small attention.

THOMAS PERCY, 1728–1811, the son of a Shropshire grocer, was educated at Oxford, entered the Church, and became Lord Bishop of Dromore, in Ireland. He very appropriately receives our notice by virtue of his *Reliques of English Poetry*, first published in 1765, and again with additions in 1794, the important influence of which has been already mentioned. Percy investigated the riches of our ballad literature, and reproduced the works of the bards and minstrels, of whom he wrote that they "were greatly respected by our ancestors, and contributed to soften the roughness of a martial and unlettered people by their songs and by their music."

These ballads are written in a style of great simplicity, and, after Bishop Percy had proclaimed their merits, received much attention from Goldsmith, Johnson, Cowper, Wordsworth, Scott, Southey, and Coleridge. In No. 70 of the *Spectator*, Addison had long before expressed his interest in the songs of the common people, and other writers had praised them, but it was left for Percy to bring their great charms before the world in such a form, that all succeeding poets, even down to Tennyson, have been obliged to own their influence. Percy's works include *The Legend of King Arthur*, *St. George and the Dragon*, *Chevy Chase*, *John Anderson my Jo*, *Lilli Burlero*, *Leir*, and others illustrating Shakespeare; and the *Hermit of Warkworth*, the last being, however, the bishop's own composition. These ballads opened a fresh fountain of poetry, and among other effects, they gave the first impulse to the genius of Sir Walter Scott.

PERCY BYSSHE SHELLEY, 1792–1822, was of wealthy parentage, studious habits, but of irregular education, having been expelled from Oxford at the age of nineteen for a defense of atheism. His rich genius and enthusiastic nature were poisoned by the infidelity of Voltaire, and his poems are full of audacious skepticism, and abominable pictures in which religion is decried, and marriage is arbitrarily made productive only of misery. His chief productions are, *Queen Mab*, *Alastor, or the Spirit of Solitude*, *Revolt of Islam*, *Prometheus Unbound*, *The Cenci*, *Rosalind and Helen*, and minor poems. Among the last is the *Ode to a Skylark*, which is full of simplicity and beauty, and in which Wordsworth declared Shelley's genius culminated. Dr. Craik says that "the highest poetical genius of this time, if it was not that of Coleridge, was, probably, that of Shelley. So much poetry, so rich in various beauty, was probably never poured forth with so rapid a flow from any other mind." Of Shelley's *Epipsychidion*, written the last year of his life, the same critic asserts that it may be considered, "for its wealth and fusion of all the highest things — of imagination, of expression, of music — one of the greatest miracles ever wrought in poetry." Many of his writings are, however, disfigured by monstrous and hideous pictures for which his remarkable genius cannot atone.

Lord Byron, 1788–1824, was a congenial friend of the last named poet. He was the profligate son of an unprincipled father who abandoned his wife and child, and died soon after on the Continent. This abandoned child, George Gordon, became by the death of his grand-uncle, Lord Byron, and the owner of Newstead Abbey, in the midst of what had been Sherwood Forest. Inheriting from his mother a passionate and uncontrolled temper, and being of an eccentric and misanthropic character, Lord Byron became noted for irregularities of conduct, contempt for restraint, the companionship of talented skeptics, and for an oriental voluptuousness of imagination. He began authorship by publishing *Hours of Idleness,* which was severely criticised by the *Edinburgh Review*, in an article supposed to have been written by Lord Brougham. Byron retaliated with a satire of indiscriminate abuse, entitled *English Bards and Scotch Reviewers.* His next work was *Childe Harold's Pilgrimage*, written after a tour on the Continent. This work, which contains many poetic descriptions of the scenes through which the author passed, made Lord Byron the idol of London, where he resided for the three succeeding years. In 1814 he produced the *Giaour*, the *Bride of Abydos*, the *Corsair*, and *Lara*. These were followed by the *Siege of Corinth*, and *Parisiana*, after the production of which, having separated from his young wife, the author left England in 1816 never to return, followed by the abuse of the journals and the hisses of the people. He afterwards wrote the *Prisoner of Chillon*, *Manfred*, a tragedy, and *Don Juan*. The last is a humorous, licentious, flippant, and incomplete poem, which shows great command of versification. One of the peculiarities of Byron's poems is that the heroes are impersonations of himself, and possess his contradictory traits. His productions exerted a dangerous influence, especially upon the young and enthusiastic. They were losing their popularity, when, in 1869, attention was temporarily attracted to them by publications of the Countess Guiccioli, Mrs. Harriet Beecher Stowe and other writers.

GEORGE CRABBE, 1754–1832, an original, conscientious, matter-of-fact poet, was the son of a revenue officer of Suffolk. By the friendship of Burke, he was encouraged in his early efforts, and placed in a position of ease as a country clergyman. He was a minute student of real life, of which he produced the traits in his poems, with an unsparing pre-Raphaelism. Byron called him "Nature's sternest painter, yet the best." Under Burke's advice he published *The Library*, in 1781, which brought him many friends, and considerable renown. In 1783 the *Village* appeared. This poem had been revised by Dr. Johnson, and by it the author's fame was insured. Among his other works are, *The Newspaper*, *The Parish Register*, *The Borough*, and *Tales of the Hall.* These exhibit true pictures of English life, and are of a high moral tone.

JEREMY BENTHAM, 1748–1832, was the son of wealthy parents, who taught him to consider himself a prodigy. He was graduated at Oxford at sixteen, being the youngest who had ever taken a degree there. Becoming a writer on law and morals, he adopted the idea of Dr. Priestly, of "the greatest good to the greatest number," and founded the utilitarian school of writers on jurisprudence. He was a friend of John Quincy Adams, our minister at

London, upon whom, as well as upon many other eminent men, his views made a deep impression. His chief works are, *Letters on Usury*, *Principles of Morals and Politics*, *Theory of Punishments and Rewards*, *Public Instruction*, and *Book of Fallacies.* Notwithstanding the arrogance and assurance of Bentham's character, and the radical defects of his theories, he has exerted considerable influence in promoting the modern improvements in legislation.

SIR WALTER SCOTT, 1771–1832, who was born of respectable parents, and raised to the baronetcy on account of his writings, wrote both in the spirit of the period we are considering, and in that of the next. Beginning his long career of authorship with poetry of the most charming and romantic description, he closed it with the most remarkable series of prose romances that ever came from the hand of one man. He attended school at Edinburgh, but was not remarkable as a scholar. Throughout life Scott's reading was exceedingly general, but his favorite authors were Spenser, Shakespeare, Milton, Boccacio, Froissart, and Bishop Percy. The *Reliques* of the last author inspired him in youth with the enthusiastic love of ballads which led to the production of the *Border Minstrelsy.* The ballads in this collection were partly original, but chiefly gathered in southern Scotland. Before the publication of the *Border Minstrelsy*, Scott had made some translations from the then fashionable German poets. The *Lay of the Last Minstrel* followed in 1805, and at later periods, *Marmion*, the *Lady of the Lake*, *Don Rod erick*, *Rokeby*, and the *Lord of the Isles*. In 1814, Scott published *Waverley*, a novel that was immediately successful, and was followed by a series produced during the next seventeen years. Of the twenty-seven novels in the *Waverley* series, twenty are historical, being founded upon events ranging from the eleventh to the eighteenth century. *Count Robert of Paris* treats of the time of the first crusade; *The Betrothed*, *The Talisman*, and *Ivanhoe*, belong to the twelfth century; *The Fair Maid of Perth* belongs to the fourteenth century; *Quentin Durward*, and *Anne of Geierstein*, are founded on French history of the fifteenth century; *The Monastery*, *The Abbot*, and *Kenilworth*, relate to the sixteenth century; the two former to Scotland, and the last to the court of Elizabeth. Five belong to the era of the seventeenth century: *The Fortunes of Nigel*, displaying London life, *The Legend of Montrose*, introducing Gustavus Adolphus, and the Thirty Years' War, *Woodstock* and *Peveril of the Peak*, relating to the times of the Cavaliers and Roundheads, and *Old Mortality*, which brings Claverhouse, and the Covenanters before us. Four belong to the eighteenth century: *Rob Roy*, which transports us to the charming Highland lakes, *The Heart of Mid-Lothian*, in which we find ourselves in Dun Edin at the time of the Porteus Mob, in the days of George II., and *Waverley* and *Redgauntlet*. This cursory review of a portion of the literary productions of Sir Walter Scott impresses us with a sense of his great diligence. Let us add to the works enumerated his *Life of Napoleon*, the *Life and Works of Dryden*, in eighteen volumes, the *Life and Works of Dean Swift*, in nine volumes, the *Tales of a Grandfather*, and novels not mentioned, and we are better able to estimate his immense labors as well as the grasp of his prolific genius. Scott expended a quarter of a million dollars on his beautiful home at Abbotsford, and when, at the age of fifty-five, he found himself involved in debts amounting to over half a million dollars, he set himself at work and paid the whole sum, actually dying in the effort. His works are familiar. They belong to the objective school, and are among the finest productions of the class. By his later works, Scott laid the foundation of the modern historical novel, and was followed by hosts of feeble writers. His works may be compared with the dramas of Shakespeare, in their variety of original characters, the historical situations, and adventures, though the dramatist, using the subjective style, displays an insight of the heart and motives which the novelist has by no means equaled.

SAMUEL TAYLOR COLERIDGE, 1772–1834, was the son of a Devonshire clergyman. He received his education chiefly at Christ's Hospital, better known as the Blue Coat School, where he began a life-long intimacy with Charles Lamb, one of his school fellows. Lamb called Coleridge, "The inspired charity boy, to whom the casual passer through the cloisters listened entranced with admiration as he unfolded with deep and sweet intonations, the mysteries of Iamblichus or Plotinus, or recited the Greek of Homer or Pindar." Beginning life as a Unitarian preacher and a visionary republican, he finally became both a royalist and a believer in the Trinity. His life and writings exhibit the influence of the speculative philosophy of Kant, Schelling, and Jacobi, as well as of the poetic art of Goethe and Schiller, names which represent the revival of German literature. Professor Shedd, in an edition of Coleridge's works published in New York in 1853, has contributed much to give a clear view of this author's real character. The distressing habit of opium-eating became his master, and caused his sun to go down in a cloud that for a score of years had hung over him. Coleridge was wonderful as a conversationist, a singularly rare accomplishment in his day. He is known as the author of *Christabel*, *Genevieve*, the *Rime of the Ancient Mariner*, *Ode to Mont Blanc*, *Lectures on Shakespeare*, the *Statesman's Manual*, and *Aids to Reflection*. Coleridge belonged to the Lake School. His works are all fragmentary, but he is admired as a critic, poet, philosopher, and divine.

CHARLES LAMB, 1775–1834, was a nervous and

thoughtful boy, the son of a Londoner of humble circumstances, and after receiving his education in the Blue Coat School, became a clerk in the office of the East India Company. After standing behind the desk of the accountant thirty-three years, Lamb was retired on a pension. He never married, but devoted himself, with a noble spirit of self-sacrifice, to the care of an insane sister. His favorite books were the works of Beaumont and Fletcher, Massinger, Jeremy Taylor, Sir Thomas Browne, Thomas Fuller, and others of the old school. Lamb's works are marked by a gentle humor, and are full of quaint fancies, and original thoughts. He is chiefly known as the author of the *Essays of Elia*, originally printed in the *London Magazine.*

Thomas Arnold, 1795–1842, the distinguished master of Rugby School, was a native of the Isle of Wight, and a graduate of Oxford University. His chief reputation is as a teacher, but he is deservedly admired also as a historian, theologian, critic, and Christian scholar. Among his writings are, *Lectures on Modern History*, the *History of Rome*, the *Later Roman Commonwealth*, and some influential works on theology. Dr. Arnold's works are characterized by catholicity, varied scholarship, and discriminating taste.

Robert Southey, 1774–1843, was of humble origin, but of fair education, and became one of the most voluminous writers in the language. Beside many minor works, he published one hundred and nine volumes under his own name. He was a brother-in-law of Coleridge, and passed through the same changes of political views and religious doctrine. He resided at Keswick, among the Cumberland lakes, and is classed with the Lake poets, though lacking their simplicity and originality. He was exemplary in all the relations of life, and methodical in his literary labors. His numerous works are the result of vast research, and exhibit wide reading. Southey wrote both in prose and verse, and among his productions are, *Joan of Arc*, an epic poem, *Wat Tyler*, *Thalaba*, *Madoc*, *The Curse of Kehama*, *Roderick the Last of the Goths*, *The Vision of Judgment*, *Life of Nelson*, *Colloquies on Society*, *The Doctor*, and *History of the Peninsular War*.

THOMAS CAMPBELL, 1777–1844, was the son of a Scottish merchant, and was educated at the University of Glasgow. He is known as the author of *Pleasures of Hope*, *Hohenlinden*, *Ye Mariners of England*, *Gertrude of Wyoming*, *The Last Man*, *Lord Ullin's Daughter*, and a variety of prose works. His poems were highly esteemed by Sir Walter Scott, and bear the marks of taste, refinement, pure moral sentiment, sublimity, and enthusiasm.

THOMAS HOOD, 1798–1845, deserves mention as

the greatest wit and humorist of his age. He was a native of London, and the son of a book-seller. His writings in prose and verse are of pure morals, and generally have a philanthropic or humane design. Hood's first work was *Whims and Oddities*, which made him popular at once. Subsequently he produced the *Bridge of Sighs*, *Eugene Aram*, the *Song of the Shirt*, and many other compositions of great popularity and geniality.

SYDNEY SMITH, 1771–1845, the first editor of the *Edinburgh Review*, was an English divine, and the son of a gentleman of eccentric habits. He took his degree of B. A. at Oxford in 1792. Possessing the humor and some other of the traits of Dean Swift, Sydney Smith has exercised a good temper, which is in contrast with the cynicism of the former writer, and which has endeared him to his readers. In addition to his contributions to the *Review*, Smith published *Letters on the Subject of the Catholics*, which are full of drollery; *Letters to Archdeacon Singleton*, and *Letters on the Pennsylvania Bonds*. He had been a eulogist of America, but in the last mentioned letters he used his humor and power of invective in exhibiting the subject of repudiation in the light under which it appeared to him, a holder of some of the bonds referred to. There is a levity and worldliness in Smith's writings hardly becoming a clergyman, though his life appears to have been pure, and his acts correct, and he is by no means so offensive as Dean Swift.

EDGAR ALLAN POE, 1811–1849, was the dissipated son of an actor and actress, who both died, leaving him an orphan at the age of four years. Edgar was then adopted and educated by a wealthy merchant of Baltimore, Maryland. He is best known as the author of the *Raven*, a poem of weird horror; and by his vigorous, quaint, melodramatic, and sombre tales and sketches. *Annabel Lee*, is a poetical lament over his dead wife, and is esteemed one of the sweetest lyrics in the language.

WILLIAM WORDSWORTH, 1770–1850, was born and lived among the beauties of those romantic lakes of northwestern England, of which we have already spoken. He delighted to contemplate every change in the varying beauties of nature, and to express his passionate love in simple words. The opinions of the highest critics were at first unfavorable to the style of the Lake School, but Sir Walter Scott and the poet Rogers gave their approval. After passing through several stages of criticism the efforts of Wordsworth are now appreciated, and his faults are recognized as the natural concomitants of such a reform as he labored for. Among Wordsworth's works are, *The Excursion*, *The White Doe of Rylstone*, *Ruth*, *We are Seven*, *Lines on Revisiting the Wye*, *Peter Bell*, and *Lyrical Ballads*. Archbishop Trench regards his *Lines suggested by a Picture of Peele Castle in a Storm*, as the highest expression of his genius.

Daniel Webster, 1782–1852, the greatest American statesman, was born among the granite hills of New Hampshire. He was educated in the common school, at Exeter Academy, and Dartmouth College. Beginning to practice law, and becoming a Federalist in politics, he soon rose to eminence, and was sent to represent his native State in the federal House of Representatives. He was afterwards for many years a prominent member of the United States Senate, and at last became Secretary of State. As an orator he was vigorous, manly, and eloquent. As a writer he has been said to have united in his productions perspicuity, beauty, precision, and strength. His works have been published in six volumes, with a life by Edward Everett. Among his orations are those entitled *The Principal Maxims of Washington's Administration*, *The First Settlement of New England*, *Discourse in Commemoration of Jefferson and Adams*, *Reply to Hayne*, *Address on laying the Corner Stone of Bunker Hill Monument*, and others. His is another of the great minds which have found strength and nourishment in the books of the Bible.

Thomas Moore, 1779–1852, was a native of Dublin, of Roman Catholic parentage, and of classical education. He was a constant frequenter of the gayest society of London, and an intimate friend of Lord Byron. After enjoying some governmental patronage, which gave him an opportunity to visit America, and finally involved him in pecuniary disaster, he devoted himself to literature as a profession. Among his best known works are, *Lalla Rookh*, a series of Oriental tales in verse; *Irish Melodies*, the *Loves of the Angels*, and the *Life of Byron.* Moore has the reputation of a devoted husband, loving father, affectionate son, and firm friend, though his writings are superficial and not of a high moral tone. Lord Jeffrey very pithily calls him "the most licentious of modern versifiers, and the most poetical of the propagators of immorality."

SAMUEL ROGERS, 1763–1855, produced poems during the entire period now under consideration. He was the son of a banker, to which business he was himself bred, and in which he accumulated wealth. His home in St. James Place, London, was a constant resort for many famous men and women, among whom were Fox, Erskine, Grattan, Sheridan, Mackintosh, Wellington, Byron, Moore, Campbell, Scott, Irving, Wordsworth, Sydney Smith, Madame de Staël, and others. Rogers was himself carefully educated, and his poems are marked by refinement rather than force. He delighted to befriend struggling merit, and to indulge his genial charity. His chief works are, *Pleasures of Memory*, *Human Life*, *Columbus*, and *Italy*.

A review of this period reveals a richness in works of a poetical and romantic nature, and a unity of character among the writers, not found in any other age. Thomas Percy, who heads the list, did not die until Samuel Rogers, who closes it, was forty-five years old, and to a great extent the whole group of authors was contemporary. It is possible that with the exception of Poe they should all have met at different times at the hospitable board of the poet Rogers.

We can readily imagine the enthusiastic Percy hailing with pleasure the budding of poetic genius as it appeared in Shelley, Byron, Crabbe, Scott, Coleridge, Southey, Campbell, Hood, Wordsworth, and Rogers, and rejoicing in the elegant prose and romance of Bentham and Scott; and it is no stretch of the imagination when we figure to ourselves the dignified orator of the Occident entertained by the Nestor of St. James Place, or think of any of the kindred spirits we have mentioned, receiving from the same patron encouragement and sympathy in those times of doubt or darkness, when fellow-feeling is just the thing to be prized. Nor can we forget the blessedness of giving that a poet of such wealth experiences in unostentatiously and delicately helping his less favored fellows.

Let us look again at some of the accumulations of the period. We are bewildered by the view as the fanciful *Elia* hands us his quaint *Essays* from the dingy East India House; as the banker-poet presents us his richly adorned volumes from St. James Place; as the historian of the early ballads calls to us from the home of the Percys to admire the story of King Cophetua who loved the beggar maid; as the historical romances of Scott turn our thoughts to his turreted home at Abbotsford; as the titled proprietor of Newstead Abbey tells us the story of *Childe Harold;* as the wild, poetic notes of Shelley's muse mingle with the pure nature-tones of the simple Wordsworth in the breezes from the lakes; as the venerable rector of Trowbridge repeats, with his characteristic minuteness, the story of sweet Phœbe Dawson as she tripped so gayly over the village green!

The romance and the poetry of this age verily drew their inspiration from varied sources, and were moulded amid varied scenes. It is a pleasure as we mark their development, to reflect that so much is pure and of good report. The hand of Time is drawn over the dark blots in the picture, and they grow less and less distinct, while we see more and more of the transcendent beauties which mark the development of the poetic element in our loved literature!

CHAPTER XIV.

MATURE ENGLISH.

Influence of the People, 1700–1870.

IV. AGE OF PROSE ROMANCE, 1830–1870.

N the twenty-sixth of June, 1830, there died in England one of whom the late Duke of Wellington wrote, "He was indeed the most extraordinary compound of talent, wit, buffoonery, obstinacy, and good feeling — in short, a medley of the most opposite qualities, with a great preponderance of good — that I ever saw in any character in my life." Such was George IV., judged by one only seven years his junior, who had long been acquainted with his character.

One month later the city of Paris was shaken to its centre. It was Monday morning, the twenty-sixth of July, that the populace in the French capital began to cry "Down with the Ministers!" On Tuesday the cry in the streets was louder and bolder. "Up with Liberty! Down with the Bourbons!" was distinctly heard, and M. Guizot recorded that there was "a revolutionary and unchained insurrection." On Wednesday Paris was declared in a state of siege; the Rue St. Antoine was barricaded; there was a desperate fight about the Hôtel de Ville; the street lamps were put out at night; no mail nor diligence was permitted to leave the city; several hundred men lay dead in the streets; and in the midst of the commotion, the King of France, Charles X., passed the evening playing cards in his palace. Thursday came, and the working-men, who had borne the brunt of the battle the day before, found their ranks increased by many of the National Guard, young students, and some deputies. Six thousand barricades had been formed in the thoroughfares, of planks, carts, paving-stones, furniture, and even piano-fortes. Everywhere battle raged. During the day the Louvre and the Tuileries were captured. Charles X. was informed that the royal family had ceased to reign, and he hastily left Paris. On Friday, July 30, the administration was offered to Louis Philippe, Duke of Orleans, was accepted, and order was restored. The tricolor waved from every building, and the Bourbons were expelled from France.

If we could have looked upon the Parliament of Great Britain just before and just after the death of King George IV., we should have heard much excited debate about reform. For nearly half a century there had been debate of the same kind — since the days of Pitt, in fact; and a year after the last of the Georges left the world, a reform bill, proposed by Lord John Russell, was actually passed.

The Tories, who strove to curb the power of the people, gave way to the Whigs, who strove to curb the power of the crown.

In 1825 a railway was begun between Liverpool and Manchester, and in 1830 a steam locomotive was first used upon it. In the summer of the same year the first American steam locomotive, which had been made under the direction of Horatio Allen in West Street, New York, was placed upon the rails. Since that date the whole continent has echoed the whistle of the locomotive, and railways have spread throughout the civilized world. Since that date, too, the electric telegraph, from feeble beginnings, has advanced, until to-day the most popular literature is that which brings to our door the daily news of all quarters of the globe, as the joint fruit of the printing-press, the electric-telegraph, and the steam locomotive.

We have had occasion to notice the intimate relations which have existed between Italy, France, Germany, England, and our own country, in the influences which each nation has exerted at one time and another upon the others of the group. The Italian Revival of Letters of the fifteenth century had an influence upon all Europe, and we have seen that it left no slight mark upon our literature. The French in the days of the Grand Monarque gave us an impetus in another direction at the period of the Restoration. When Goethe, who has been called the greatest literary artist of the nineteenth century, arose in Germany, a more impassioned style of thought and sentiment was promoted by his influence on our writers, especially during the period of poetical romance.

We now come to the days of prose romance, and ask, what influences have been put forth during the last forty years? Where have they originated, and what marks have they made?

A survey of the field shows that about the year 1830, there was a general impulse given to education and freedom in France, England, and the United States, and also that there was a simultaneous political excitement in those countries, having apparently different causes. There was a general breaking up of old ways of thinking and feeling, and literature, which grows out of men's thoughts and feelings, and depends to a considerable extent upon social and political affairs, sympathized with these changes, and was affected by them.

We have already seen that the year was marked by the elevation of the Orleans dynasty in France, and if we search the annals of that country, we shall find that the new ruler made, among other movements the same year, those which have resulted in the present liberal system of education in that country. During Louis Philippe's reign, also, laws were enacted abolishing slavery in his dominions, though these were not thoroughly enforced until a later period. The changes in France also exerted an influence in favor of the downfall of Toryism in England, of which we have spoken.

In Germany the writers who followed Göthe not only exhibit the influence of his wonderful genius, but also bear the impress of that study of philosophy of which Schelling was a prominent exponent. The political excitement in France, which has been referred to, was one cause of a new and more strictly romantic literary feeling in Germany, evident in the class of authors called "New Germany," and in the so-called "Romantic School." The skepticism of Hume gave rise to philosophical discussions in Germany by Kant and his followers, from which resulted a new influence felt in England by many authors of the present century, especially apparent in the writings of Coleridge, Carlyle, and Emerson. Referring to the influence of modern German literature upon our own, Dr. Craik says that in the earlier part of the present century it was entirely confined to a certain class or school of writers in verse. "But now," he continues, "that in the middle period of the century prose has taken the place which in the last age belonged to verse, this latest foreign affection which has seized upon our literature has naturally acquired a much more extended range."

In England the present generation is more enlightened in every respect than any former one has been, and for very good reasons. The passage of the Reform Bill, which has been mentioned, was followed in 1833 by the first public grant in that country in behalf of public education. Since that date such grants have become regular items in the expenses of government, and have very largely increased. There were never so many good schools in England as there are to-day, and the number of students and general readers is constantly augmenting. The same year, 1833, also witnessed the passage of a bill definitely abolishing negro slavery in Great Britain.

Turning now to our own country, we find that at the beginning of our period, Andrew Jackson had just entered upon his first term of office as President, after a protracted and violent political campaign. The year 1830 saw the revival of the excitement on the subject of slavery, which had raged with so much fury in 1819–20, when the State of Missouri was admitted to the Union. After ten years of comparative though not entire quiet on this subject, during which Benjamin Lundy, a Quaker, zealously espoused the cause of the oppressed, a new anti-slavery journal was begun in 1831, by William Lloyd Garrison, under the title of *The Liberator*, advocating immediate emancipation. The excitement on this subject was thereafter continuous until the enfranchisement of the blacks, by proclamation of President Lincoln. The march of intelligence in the United States during this period has never been paralleled, and could hardly have been conceived by the wisest of any previous century.

This remarkable increase of intelligence has caused a notable increase in the number of readers, and in the average knowledge of the people, in France, England, and the United States during the present period. There has been also an increase of the number of thinkers in these lands, but the latter class by no means increases in an equal ratio with the former. It is necessary to bear this fact constantly in mind as we scrutinize the development of our age in literary affairs.

It may not be true that the greatest number of our inhabitants would be found in the lowest class, if ranked according to scholarly acquirements, but it is quite true that the highest classes in such a scale, would be found to contain the fewest individuals. It is therefore to be expected that the books of the greatest erudition should have the smallest number of readers, while sensational, smart, startling, conceited, and empty writing will be popular and profitable at once.

This train of reasoning may be easily pursued by the reader. The fact stated will operate unfavorably to the highest development of the best pure literature at any age, when authors must write for a popular demand. It is pleasant, therefore, to be able to add that among the annually increasing number of superficial readers, there always is an increasing number, who from various causes are developing into thinkers, and who will of course encourage thoughtful writers. These need to study the very best literature of the past and present, to become familiar with it, and to learn to love that in it which is the most exalted, and the purest in style and sentiment.

Before the publication of Sir Walter Scott's *Waverley Novels*, the spirit of our literature was deeply poetical. Since that time literature has expressed itself more in the form of prose, and no department of prose writing has during the last forty years so greatly flourished as the prose romance. We need only remember the works of Irving, Cooper, Bulwer, Hawthorne, Thackeray, Dickens, Reade, and others to appreciate this truth.

The steam locomotive, which began to roll its wheels with this period, is an appropriate emblem of the progress that marks our age. We have advanced in that the new element of female authorship has become more prominent in our literature, — a very interesting fact that can only be hinted in our brief notice of the authors of the day. We exhibit our progress in greater attention to finish and grammatical perfection, while unfortunately, we have left behind some of the spontaneity that was charming in the last age.

Since the beginning of this era, there has been greater political tranquillity than during those which have preceded it, and the opportunity has been embraced of making investigations in the domains of history, physical science, politics, philosophy, and art. The periodical literature of our generation is developed far beyond that of past days. In this direction writers have produced the solid quarterly review, the entertaining monthly magazine, and the gossipy daily and weekly news journals. The first gives us a considerate, and generally a trustworthy literary guide. The magazine furnishes a pleasant companion, and sometimes an instructive popular teacher. The news journal presents a photograph of the world's doings, with all its good, bad, and indifferent traits brought into prominence. The literary weekly journal too frequently contains little more than such feeble or sensational novels as create a temporary excitement, and impoverish the reader's mind, or give crude or false pictures of life and duty. The great pecuniary success of some of this class of journals is an alarming token of the superficiality of the mass of the minds of the period. On the other side, it must be added that the vastly increased circulation of solid works of a historical, doctrinal, or philosophical nature must be accepted as a favorable token.

Mention has already been made of some of the American writers of this generation ; and it is only necessary to add that they have made advance in every line of literary activity, and command universal attention. The world's libraries are nowhere perfect in our day without a large infusion of the American element. To a greater extent our authors strive to create a national spirit in their productions, a fact that will be apparent as we consider the individual writers.[1]

[1] While the authors in former periods have been arranged in the order of their death, in the present chapter they are, for obvious reasons, inserted in the order of their birth.

WALTER SAVAGE LANDOR, 1775–1864, was the son of a gentleman of good family and considerable wealth. He pursued studies at Rugby and Oxford, but was insubordinate at both places, and never took a degree. Though his character was as inconsistent and contradictory as that of his sovereign, George IV., and exerted much influence upon his writings, they are not deficient in earnestness and importance. Landor's works are marked by genius, but also by rashness, wilfulness, and ungoverned passion. They are in parts graceful, polished, and scholarly, in parts inconsiderate, paradoxical, and offensive to good taste. He is known as a prose writer chiefly by his *Imaginary Conversations of Literary Men and Statesmen*, and *Pericles and Aspasia*. Among his poems are, *Heroic Idyls*, and *Gebir, Count Julian, and other Poems.*

HENRY HALLAM, 1778–1859, one of the most judicious historians of a period noted for the care with which historical studies have been pursued, was educated at Eton School and at Oxford University. Enjoying a competent income, he devoted himself to a line of critical study in which he had no predecessor in England. He was one of the editors of the *Edinburgh Review.* His chief works are, *A View of the State of Europe in the Middle Ages*, *Constitutional History of England from the Accession of Henry VII. to the Death of George II.*, and an *Introduction to the Literature of Europe in the*

Fifteenth, Sixteenth, and Seventeenth Centuries. These are standard works of the most painstaking, original investigation, and are marked by fairness, terseness, and perspicacity in their presentation of opinions, and discussions of principles. Lord Macaulay styled the *Constitutional History* the most impartial book he had ever read.

Henry, Lord Brougham, 1778–1869, was of an ancient family, educated at the University of Edinburgh, the city of his birth, and was at an early age distinguished for his investigations in physics and mathematics. For many years he was prominent as a statesman, using his influence in behalf of popular education and the abolition of the slave-trade. Among his writings are, *Sketches of Statesmen who flourished in the Time of George III.*, *Lives of Men of Letters and Science who flourished in the Time of George III.*, *Political Philosophy*, *Speeches on Social and Political Subjects*, and a dissertation entitled *Analytical and Experimental Inquiries on the Cells of Bees.* Two of his speeches on the occasion of the trial of Queen Caroline in 1820 and 1821, have taken an honorable place among the specimens of classic English oratory.

Washington Irving, 1783–1859, sometimes called the American Goldsmith, and whose writings remind us of Sir Walter Scott, was a native of New York city. After receiving a good school education he began the study of law, which he soon relinquished for authorship. In 1807, in connection with his friend, James Kirke Paulding, he projected a serial entitled *Salmagundi*, in which the humors of the town were set off in a popular way. This was continued through twenty numbers. In 1809, Irving published *A History of New York, from the Beginning of the World to the End of the Dutch Dynasty, by Diedrich Knickerbocker*, which was a humorous description of the author's native city under the Dutch governors. Among his numerous other works are, *The Sketch Book*, *Bracebridge Hall*, *Tales of a Traveller*, *Life of Columbus*, *Conquest of Granada*, *Tales of the Alhambra*, *Abbotsford and Newstead Abbey*, *Astoria*, *Life of Goldsmith*, *Mahomet*, *Wolfert's Roost*, and *Life of Washington*. These are written in a pure, flowing, simple style, and are enriched by dashes of humor and scintillations of wit.

James Henry Leigh Hunt, 1784–1859, a schoolfellow of Coleridge and Lamb, and a friend of Byron, Shelley, and Keats, was a descriptive poet of original genius, and an essayist of delicate fancy. After having been associated with his brother John, in conducting a paper called *The News*, Leigh Hunt joined him in establishing *The Examiner*, a weekly publication, the independent spirit of which attracted much attention. This paper turns our thoughts back to the days of Charles Lamb, for Hunt formed one of the congenial circle which rendered so attractive the Wednesday evening receptions of the author of the *Essays of Elia.* United by similarity of literary and political taste, and suspected of ulterior designs, Godwin, Hunt, Hazlitt, Wordsworth, Southey, and Coleridge frequently met at the rooms of Lamb to play whist and to discuss politics, art, and literature, as well as to give expression to friendly sympathy. The *Examiner* criticised the measures of government very freely, and at last, for a too truthful picture of George IV., the proprietors were heavily fined and thrown into prison. The story of the two years of Leigh Hunt's imprisonment is an interesting one; for he was the object of much attention from his many literary friends, and he enlivened his solitary hours by indulging in poetical composition. His later years were passed in the pleasant companionship of his friends (among whom Carlyle and the Brownings were then numbered), and in cheerful studies, the fruit of which is apparent in the wide range and desultory character of his later writings. Among his poems are, *Captain Sword and Captain Pen*, and the *Story of the Rimini.* His essays are included in a volume entitled *The Indicator and the Companion, a Miscellany for the Fields and the Fireside.*

THOMAS DE QUINCEY, 1786–1859, one of the most peculiar and voluminous authors of the period, was the son of a merchant of Manchester, and a graduate of Oxford. For fourteen years he was a slave to opium, and his best-remembered work is entitled *Confessions of an English Opium Eater.* Like Coleridge, who had the same habit, De Quincey, though one of the greatest masters of English prose of the century, was a fitful worker, and some of his most brilliant conceptions were left uncompleted. Among his other writings are, *The Flight of the Kalmuck Tartars,* and *Murder considered as one of the Fine Arts.*

RICHARD WHATELY, 1787–1863, late Archbishop of Dublin, was one of the most active and influential writers of the period. In treating religious topics he is characterized by a peculiar charity and catholicity, and he is distinguished also by a thorough acquaintance with the subjects he discusses, and by great clearness of style. Among his works are, *Elements of Logic, Elements of Rhetoric, Lectures on Political Economy, Annotations on Bacon's Essays,* and on *Paley's Moral Philosophy.*

SIR WILLIAM HAMILTON, 1788–1856, a native of Glasgow and a graduate of Oxford, was a profound thinker, a great philosopher, and a clear writer. Among his works are an edition of Dr. Reid's works, and *Discussions on Philosophy,* which latter are said to contain a more exhaustive analysis of the intellectual processes than the work of any other English writer.

JAMES FENIMORE COOPER, 1789–1851, the voluminous American novelist, was of English descent, a native of New Jersey, and a resident at Cooperstown, New York. With bold self-reliance this author produced novels based upon the fresh romantic materials of his native country. He depicted the backwoodsman, the prairie-hunter, the aboriginal red man, the vicissitudes of pioneer life, and the scenes of Indian warfare, with a picturesque pen, and in a national spirit. Among his works are, *Precaution*, *The Spy*, *Last of the Mohicans*, *The Prairie*, *The Pathfinder*, *Deerslayer*, *The Pilot*, *History of the United States Navy*, *Gleanings in Europe*, and *Sketches in Switzerland*. His novels number more than thirty, are of unequal merit, and bear evidence of haste and sometimes of carelessness. They are distinctively American, and were a means of rendering Europeans familiar with American scenes.

JOHN KEBLE, 1790–1866, received his early education from his venerated father, and was thus prepared, as he was also by nature, to form his judgments, "not by reason or argument, but by authority." In 1827 he published his most celebrated work, *The Christian Year*, or thoughts in verse for the Sundays and holidays throughout the year, which exhibited marked poetic genius, and has since passed through a hundred editions. Though designed for the English Church, its reception has illustrated the fact, that the words of the true poet often possess a wider significance than he himself is conscious of; for it has proved a favorite with devout Christians of all communions. From 1833 to 1844, Keble was Professor of Poetry at Oxford University. His life, which has been compared with that of "holy George Herbert," was, however, mainly passed in the unobtrusive and assiduous performance of his duties as a parish clergyman. He exerted a gentle, yet powerful influence upon men of letters, bringing the charms of poetry and the greatest purity of life, to the aid of what has been termed the Oxford, or High-Church movement in the English Church, which commenced in 1833. In this he was associated with Newman, Pusey, and others, and to it Keble contributed some of the most important of the *Tracts for the Times*. Among his other works are, *Lyra Innocentium*, and an edition of the *Works of Richard Hooker*, author of *Ecclesiastical Polity*. His language is frequently too classical to be popular.

William Cullen Bryant, 1794– ——, a native of the little mountain town of Cummington in western Massachusetts, was directed in early youth by a judicious and cultured father to detect and avoid a false poetic enthusiasm, and to appreciate the value of correctness and compression. His father encouraged his youthful aspirations, and was rewarded by evidence of early maturity. At a time when the artificial style of Pope was highly extolled.

young Bryant obtained some of Wordsworth s ballads. These had probably an influence on his future, and fixed him in his love of those pure and national subjects which touch the heart. Among Bryant's poems are, *Thanatopsis*, *Death of the Flowers*, *Ode to the Connecticut River*, *The Forest Hymn*, *The Indian Girl's Lament*, *The Song of Marion's Men*, a translation of *Homer's Iliad;* and he has written a large number of prose compositions, essays, letters, and political papers, marked by pure and vigorous English. Mr. Bryant is now one of the editors and proprietors of the New York *Evening Post.*

THOMAS CARLYLE, 1795-——, is the son of a Scotch farmer. He is highly educated, being a graduate of the University of Edinburgh, and in his youth was a companion of the gifted and erratic Edward Irving. Carlyle has drawn inspiration from the German metaphysicians who so greatly influenced Coleridge and other English thinkers. Being original and audacious, and using the German style, Mr. Carlyle's works are marked by complex conceits which are not generally approved. In the words of a late writer, the critical and biographical essays of Carlyle first familiarized Englishmen with the riches of modern German thought. "For this work, he was incomparably better fitted than any man then living in Britain. Possessing a knowledge of the German tongue such as no foreigner ever surpassed, he was also inspired by the conviction that the literature of Germany, in depth, truthfulness, sincerity, and earnestness of purpose, was greatly superior to what was admired and relished at home. Gifted, moreover, in a degree altogether unexampled, with a talent for portraiture, he soon painted on the British memory the images of Schiller, Fichte, Jean Paul Richter, and other foreign magnates, until then almost unheard of." His peculiarities, being those of a bold writer with a strong purpose and honest convictions, deserve at least respectful criticism by those who may not be entirely in accord with the most advanced positions he assumes. His chief works are, *Life of Schiller*, *Sartor Resartus*, *Essays*, *The French Revolution*, *Frederick the Great*, *Hero Worship*, etc.

FRANCIS WAYLAND, 1796–1865, a native of New York city, a graduate of Union College and of Andover Seminary, and for twenty-five years President of Brown University, was the author of a number of works distinguished for independence, thoroughness, and perspicuity. He is chiefly known as the writer of works on *Moral Science*, *Political Economy*, and *Intellectual Philosophy*. These works have given their author a solid and wide-spread reputation.

WILLIAM HICKLING PRESCOTT, 1796–1859, was a grandson of one of the American commanders at the battle of Bunker Hill. He was born at Salem graduated at Harvard, and intended for the study of law, from which he was debarred by an affection of the eyes. Using the eyes of others in his investigations, he became a historian, and produced in succession the *History of Ferdinand and Isabella, Conquest of Mexico, Conquest of Peru*, and *History of the Reign of Philip II.* These are all works of laborious original research. The first mentioned was immediately received with great praise in England, and was translated into German, Italian, French, and Spanish, and, no less than all of Prescott's writings, is a standard work. The style is elevated, simple, firm, and dignified.

MARK HOPKINS, 1802-——, is a native of Stockbridge, Massachusetts, graduated at Williams College with the highest honors, and since 1836 has been the president of that institution. His chief works are, *Lectures on the Evidences of Christianity, Miscellaneous Essays and Discourses, Lectures on Moral Science, Baccalaureates*, and *The Law of Love and Love as a Law.* The president's Baccalaureate sermon delivered in 1869 is entitled *Spirit and Soul and Body*, a discourse on the tripartite nature of man. Dr. Hopkins' works are marked by eloquence, practical philosophy, and the apt application of sound principles in morals and religion.

RALPH WALDO EMERSON, 1803-——, is a native of Boston, and a graduate of Harvard University. He entered the ministry of the Unitarian Church, but his course of thought rapidly led him away from systems of theology and ecclesiastical organizations, and the boldness of his attitude in all discussions of religion and philosophy, together with the fascination of his poetic nature, made him the chief person in a knot of enthusiastic men and women who essayed to make fresh statements of religious and social problems. Emerson's prose and poetry are alike marked by a certain clearness of insight rather than severity of logic ; he is impatient of consistency, and prefers to say distinctly what he thinks he sees now, without much caring to make comparison with previous opinion. He is brilliant and epigrammatic in his prose, using vigorous English, and his poetry is often marked by a very beautiful interpretation of recondite facts in nature and life. His writings are unintelligible to many readers, but he has exerted a strong influence over his contemporaries of the same school. His contempt for authority, and his confidence in the sufficiency of each individual, have led him to a pantheistic belief, and to refer the sacred writings of all nations to a common source, with equal claims upon the respect of mankind. His chief published works are, *Man Thinking*, *Literary Ethics*, *The Method of Nature*, *New England Reformers*, *Poems*, *Representative Men*, *Conduct of Life*, and *Society and Solitude.*

NATHANIEL HAWTHORNE, 1804–1864, was a native of Salem, Massachusetts, a fellow-student with Longfellow, and, like that poet, a graduate of Bowdoin College. He led for many years the life of a recluse, and even when occupying positions under government in Salem, and afterward as consul at Liverpool, he entered but little into active life. He was nevertheless a most acute while silent observer of men, and his mind turned constantly toward the deep and dark problems of human nature. The sombre life of early New England had a strong fascination for him, and he has left many pictures of it, drawn from the study of history. His works discover a profound sympathy with mental suffering, a mournful curiosity respecting the more hidden springs of human action, sometimes morbid and painful, and a delicate susceptibility to the indistinct emotions. His style is exceedingly graceful, and a gentle humor plays upon the surface of all his writings, rendering the books very fascinating in their art, while often painful in subject. The *Passages from Hawthorne's Note Books*, of which the American and English portions have thus far been published, edited by his widow, show the finished character of all his studies, and the closeness of his observation. Among Hawthorne's works are, *Twice-Told Tales*, *Mosses from an Old Manse*, *The Scarlet Letter*, *The House of the Seven Gables*, *Wonder-Book for Boys and Girls*, *The Snow Image and other Twice-Told Tales*, *The Marble Faun*, and *Our Old Home, A Series of English Sketches*

EDWARD BULWER, LORD LYTTON, 1805–1873, was a native of Norfolk, England, and a graduate of Cambridge University. He was carefully nurtured by an accomplished mother, and after graduation rambled on foot through various parts of England and Scotland, and made a tour of France on horseback. He was early charmed by the old romances of the Round Table, and recounted their legends in an epic poem of considerable merit, entitled *King Arthur.* He has written several plays which are popular in the theatres, of which are, *Richelieu,* and *The Lady of Lyons.* Among his other works are, *Rienzi, The Last Days of Pompeii, The Siege of Granada, My Novel, The Caxtons,* and *What will he do with it?* His fame rests mainly upon his later novels, which are in marked contrast with his earlier works. The books produced before their author had matured, are losing their place in literature on account of their loose morals, which are offensive to pure taste. He has long been a prominent statesman, and during a creditable political career, has delivered some finished speeches.

HENRY WADSWORTH LONGFELLOW, 1807–——, is a native of Portland, Maine, a graduate of Bowdoin College, and a versatile and voluminous poet. Among his prose writings are *Outre Mer* and *Hyperion.* In verse he has produced, *Voices of the Night, The Spanish Student, The Golden Legend, Evangeline, The Song of Hiawatha, The Courtship of Miles*

Standish, *Tales of a Wayside Inn*, *The New England Tragedies*, and translations of Dante's poems. All of Longfellow's writings bear marks of his scholarship, fancy, taste, and loving heart, without any traces of pedantry. His works are probably more extensively circulated and read than those of any other American poet. They are very popular in Europe, and have thus become household words on both sides of the sea.

JOHN GREENLEAF WHITTIER, 1807- ——, is a native of Haverhill, and a resident at Amesbury, Massachusetts. His ancestors were of the Society of Friends, with which class the poet himself sympathizes. Without a collegiate education he became at an early age, first an editor, then a prose writer, and finally a poet of purity, patriotism, and deep feeling. Mr. Whittier's strong anti-slavery principles made him one of the foremost writers in the struggle in the United States, to which reference has been made. In support of this cause, he produced *The Voices of Freedom*, a collection of poems published in Boston in 1850, and he continued to produce verses of the same character as long as the struggle lasted. His later poems have appeared in the current periodicals, the greater number of them in the *Atlantic Monthly Magazine*. Among his prose publications are, *Legends of New England*, *Margaret Cook's Journal*, and *Literary Recreations and Miscellanies*. In verse he has written *Mogg*

Megone, *The Bridal of Pennacook*, *The Chapel of the Hermits*, *Home Ballads and Poems*, *In War Time*, *Nauhaught the Deacon*, and *Snow Bound.*

ELIZABETH BARRETT BROWNING, 1809–1861. The education of Elizabeth Barrett was conducted by her father with the most solicitous care, and included a thorough acquaintance with moral and natural philosophy, and the ancient and modern languages. After publishing *The Seraphim and other Poems* in 1838, she passed through a painful illness which confined her for years to her chamber. This affliction exerted an important influence, for the period was one of deep application, and resulted in the revision of her former poems, and in the composition of new ones. Her taste for classic studies did not forsake her, and besides the writers of Greece, she studied parts of the Old Testament in the original Hebrew. In 1846, she married Robert Browning, one of the first poets of England, and thereafter resided in Florence, Italy. Mrs. Browning's poems are not all popular, on account of their mystic and somewhat obscure nature, but they exhibit marked genius, rare delicacy of thought, intense sympathy with suffering, and indignation at injustice. Among her principal writings are, *Prometheus Bound*, *Lady Geraldine's Courtship*, *Casa Guidi Windows*, *Aurora Leigh*, and *Drama of Exile.*

OLIVER WENDELL HOLMES, 1809-——, a native

of Cambridge, Massachusetts, is a graduate of Harvard and of Dartmouth Medical College. He has written many verses that are well known, among which are, *Old Ironsides*, *The Last Leaf*, *The Height of the Ridiculous*, *My Aunt*, and *On Lending a Punch Bowl*, which are marked by pathos, playful fancy, and genial humor. He is also a prose writer, and has published *The Autocrat of the Breakfast Table*, *Elsie Venner — a Romance of Destiny*, *The Guardian Angel*, etc. In both prose and verse, perhaps the most marked characteristic of Dr. Holmes' writing is an incisive wit, which is quick to find weakness or dullness in persons or sentiment. There is a succession of epigrammatic points which dazzle the reader, and a brilliancy and originality quite unique. Personally Dr. Holmes is very popular, and one of his most prominent characteristics is the enduring love for the place of his birth, which is apparent in all his writings. Dr. Holmes has also furnished some contributions to the literature of medical science.

ALFRED TENNYSON, 1810– ——, the present poet-laureate of England, is the son of a clergyman, a native of Lincolnshire, and a graduate of Cambridge. In 1830 he began his career as a poet by the publication of *Poems chiefly Lyrical*, a volume that included *Claribel*, *Lilian*, *Mariana*, and other pieces, but which was coldly received. Two years later he published *The Lady of Shalott*, *The Miller's Daughter*, *The May Queen*, *Lady Clara Vere de Vere*, and other poems, which also created no excitement. In 1842 his *English Idyls and other Poems* appeared, and from that time his reputation rose rapidly. This last volume included the *Morte d'Arthur*, which was republished in 1870 as the *Passing of Arthur*, *The Gardener's Daughter*, *Godiva*, *St. Simeon Stylites*, *Locksley Hall*, *Sir Galahad*, *Sir Launcelot and Queen Guinevere*, etc. In 1847 these were followed by *The Princess, a Medley*, and *In Memoriam*, the latter occasioned by the death of a loved friend, a son of Hallam, the historian. In 1859, *The Idyls of the King* appeared. In 1864, *Enoch Arden*, and in 1870, *The Holy Grail*, in which last the poet returns to his long-loved Arthurian subjects. Tennyson lives for the most of his time at Farringford, a quiet retreat on the beautiful Isle of Wight. He combines the imagination of the poet with the subtlety of the metaphysician, so that while his love-songs please the sentimental, his *In Memoriam* furnishes food for thought to the meditative mind. Among the verses produced as Laureate, are lines *On the Death of Wellington*, *On the Marriage of the Prince of Wales*, on the fatal *Charge of the Light Brigade*, and *On the Opening of the International Exhibition*, which, though possessing historic interest, have some of them been severely criticised, and are of unequal poetic merit. The simplicity of Tennyson's writings, their quaintness, originality, and force of expression, as well as the richness of their fancy, recommend them to the mind and heart.

and they are highly admired wherever the English language is read or spoken.

WILLIAM MAKEPEACE THACKERAY, 1811–1863, was born at Calcutta, where his father held a civil office. He was educated at the famous Charterhouse School, London, where Crashaw the poet, Isaac Barrow, the divine, Sir William Blackstone, Joseph Addison, Sir Richard Steele, John Wesley, General Havelock, John Leech, George Grote, and many other celebrities had also been taught. With an ample fortune, Thackeray purposed following the life of an artist, but, having lost his money in speculations, he began a literary career. Among his works are, *Letters of Michael Angelo Titmarsh*, and *George Fitz-Boodle, Esq.*, *Henry Esmond*, *Vanity Fair*, *Pendennis*, *Paris Sketch Book*, *English Humorists of the Eighteenth Century*, *The Four Georges*, *The Newcomes*, and *The Virginians*. Thackeray's studies in novel-writing seem to have been largely in the works of the earliest writers of the English school, Richardson, Smollett, and Fielding, and, like them, he aimed to give a minute picture of the life of men and women about him. His novels will probably have a new value in future days, for their very close and detailed portraiture of English social life of the period. In elaborating his work he made most thorough and painstaking research into whatever matters of fact were to be illustrated. His description of scenes connected with the Battle of

Waterloo, in *Vanity Fair*, is a brilliant historical picture busy with moving life. Thackeray was a sentimentalist who concealed his sentiment under a thin veil of satire, and he had a strong indignation against every form of social meanness, manifested in his writings by a sustained use of satire, irony, and caustic pleasantry unequaled in English literature.

CHARLES DICKENS, 1812–1870, addresses to-day a more numerous and varied circle of readers than any other author. He was born at Portsmouth, and early became attached to a London paper as reporter. This occupation probably gave direction to his genius throughout his whole brilliant career. Among his earliest productions are *The Posthumous Papers of the Pickwick Club*, not only the most popular of his writings, but perhaps the most popular book of the period. It is characterized by an overflow of animal spirits, and an extravagance of humor which took the reading public by storm. Two of his novels, *Barnaby Rudge* and *Tale of Two Cities*, are connected with historic study, but the others draw their suggestions almost entirely from life in London, though the scenes of one, *Martin Chuzzlewit*, are laid partly in the United States. The characters he has most successfully drawn are taken from studies among the vagabond and eccentric elements of city life. No English writer since Shakespeare has invented so varied a range of characters. His kindliness of nature and so-called humanitarianism have led to a sympathy for the criminal, and a sentimental pity for the self-indulgent and thriftless which has been complained of. On the other hand he has made charity fashionable, and has given much sound and harmless enjoyment to his generation, for which he is to be commended. He exhibits a reverence for the Bible, though his love of caricature has led him to draw only inconsistent professors of Christianity. Among his other writings are, *Nicholas Nickleby*, *Oliver Twist*, *Dombey and Son*, *David Copperfield*, *Our Mutual Friend*, and *Christmas Stories*. Among the last the charming tale of *Boots at the Holly Tree Inn*, is greatly admired. Mr. Dickens's latest novel, entitled *The Mystery of Edwin Drood*, was left in an incomplete condition at the time of his sudden death.

HARRIET BEECHER STOWE, 1812–——, is one of the daughters of the late Rev. Dr. Lyman Beecher, and a native of Litchfield, Connecticut. At the age of twenty-one she became the wife of Professor Calvin E. Stowe, who has occupied chairs in several theological seminaries. Mrs. Stowe was already known as the writer of minor works, when in 1852, her book entitled *Uncle Tom's Cabin*, appeared. In consequence of the excitement on the subject of slavery, as well as of the merits of the story, it met unexampled success. Though some of the negro talk would not be recognized in the South, and notwithstanding other defects, the justice with which the good points of southern character are exhibited, the powers of description manifested, the pure morality and the humane purpose of this book, gave it great value, and it was sold to an extent without precedent. Among Mrs. Stowe's later works are, *Nina Gordon*, first published as *Dred*, *Agnes of Sorrento*, *The Minister's Wooing*, *The Pearl of Orr's Island*, and a work on the mysterious *Life of Lord Byron*. The last mentioned has created great excitement in England and America, causing a new discussion of Byron's pernicious life and writings.

ROBERT BROWNING, 1812-——, was born in one of the suburbs of London, is of dissenting parentage, and was educated at London University. At the age of twenty he went to Italy, where his tastes led him to study thoroughly the past and present traits of Italian life. These he saw in far different aspects from those under which travellers and students have usually observed them. His first appeal to the public which was acknowledged, was made in the drama of *Paracelsus* in 1836, since which he has produced *Sordello*, in 1840; *Pippa Passes* and other poems in a collection called *Bells and Pomegranates*, published from 1842 to 1846; *Men and Women*, in 1855; *Dramatis Personæ*, in 1864; and *The Ring and the Book*, in 1869. These exhibit great originality, power, subtlety, and depth of feeling. Mr. Browning's writings are deficient in the elements of popularity, though he stands confessedly in the front rank of English poets. Differing entirely from Tennyson, he is however his greatest rival in the estimation of thoughtful students of literature. His subjects are sometimes English, but more frequently are drawn from mediæval history, — Oriental, Italian, or Spanish scenes, while his characters bear Italian and German names. Of Mr. Browning's shorter pieces, *The Pied Piper of Hamelin*, *How they brought Good News from Ghent to Aix*, and *The Lost Leader*, are deservedly esteemed among the finest specimens of modern English poetry.

JOHN LOTHROP MOTLEY, 1814– ——, late United States Minister at the Court of St. James, is a native of Dorchester, Massachusetts, and a graduate of Harvard University. He has been a severe student, and resided in Germany at one time for the purpose of availing himself of the great advantages afforded in that country. After publishing some spirited works of minor importance, Mr. Motley produced his great histories of the *Rise of the Dutch Republic* and the *History of the United Netherlands*, which show deep research, are of picturesque style and permanent value. These have been extensively republished in other countries, and give the author a foremost rank among the most careful historians of England and America.

James Anthony Froude, 1818- ——, is a native of Devonshire, a graduate of Oxford, and an English High Churchman. Among his early writings is the *Nemesis of Faith*, a gloomy and somewhat skeptical work. He has since produced *The History of England from the Fall of Wolsey to the Death of Elizabeth*, and *Short Studies on Great Subjects*. Notwithstanding its original title the history is continued only to the date of the Spanish Armada in 1588, the object of the author having been to sketch the transition from the Catholic England of a dominant church, monasteries, and pilgrimages, to the England of progressive intelligence. Conceiving this transition period to have ended with the defeat of the Armada, Mr. Froude closes his work with the history of that event. Some portions are written in the style of Carlyle, of whom the author is an admirer. It is eloquent, rich in the results of research, exhibits great powers of generalization, is graphic and clear. In 1872-3, Mr. Froude delivered lectures in America, on the subject of England's rule in Ireland. They added little to his reputation, and led to discussions in which his accuracy as a historian was severely attacked.

John Ruskin, 1819- ——, is a native of Edinburgh, a graduate of Oxford, and a writer on art. Mr. Ruskin has exerted an important influence upon English taste and knowledge of art by his eloquent and original writings upon those subjects, though the reader is confused by his paradoxical and inconsistent statements. Having turned from the discussion of art to political economy and other topics demanding cool judgment, Mr. Ruskin has begun to lose the respect as an authority which he had previously commanded. Among his works are, *Modern Painters, their Superiority in the Art of Landscape Painting to all the Ancient Masters; Seven Lamps of Architecture, The Stones of Venice, Lectures on Architecture and Painting, Pre-Raphaelism, Sesame and Lilies, Giotto and his Works, Ethics of the Dust,* etc. These are marked by beauty of expression, originality, eloquence, and brilliancy. combined with enthusiasm in the propagation of the author's ideas.

JAMES RUSSELL LOWELL, 1819– ——, is a native of Cambridge, and a graduate of Harvard, in which university he is a professor. His writings in prose and verse are serious, humorous, satirical, and imaginative. Among his prose works are, *Conversations on some Old Poets,* Papers in the *North American Review, Fireside Travels* and *Among My Books,* a collection of essays. In verse he has published *The Biglow Papers,* a satire directed against war and slavery; *A Fable for Critics, Vision of Sir Launfal,* from the Round Table Romances, and *The Cathedral.* He was editor of the *North American Review,* and contributed critical articles of the highest order to it, and to other current publications.

"George Eliot," 1820– ——, is the pseudonym of Mrs. Marian (Evans) Lewes, who appeared as a novelist in 1858, with *Adam Bede.* This was followed by *The Mill on the Floss* (1859) ; *Silas Marner*, and *Scenes in Clerical Life* (1861) ; *Romola*, (1864) ; *Felix Holt* (1866) ; and *Middlemarch* (1872). She is, since the deaths of Thackeray, Dickens, and Bulwer, ranked by many first among living novelists, and her works are certainly remarkable for strong and lifelike delineation of character. They are full of paragraphs apt for quotation, which embody sentiments almost in the style of the epigram. In marked contrast is Mrs. Dinah Maria (Muloch) Craik (1826– ——), whose first novel, *The Ogilvies*, appeared in 1846, and was followed by *John Halifax, Gentleman* (1856), *Christian's Mistake, A Noble Life, Mistress and Maid*, and others of a style of thought and execution more womanly than that of George Eliot. Younger and still different in style, is Miss Jean Ingelow (1830– ——), whose *Poems* breathe a spirit of purity, and elevated sentiment, and whose novel, *Off the Skelligs* (1872), became popular immediately upon its publication. These all differ from Charlotte (Brontë) Nicholls (1816–1855), author of *Jane Eyre* (1847), a novel in some degree autobiographic, of remarkable vigor, and absorbing interest. These examples show how woman is now pushing her way to the foremost rank in the literary world, and give promise that she will win brighter laurels, in this, one of her most legitimate spheres of action.

MATTHEW ARNOLD, 1822-——, is the eldest son of the celebrated Dr. Thomas Arnold of Rugby. He is a graduate of Oxford, is known as a poet of classic tastes, and as a literary critic of the French school, of which Sainte-Beuve, lately deceased, was the most prominent representative. Among his works are, *The Strayed Revellers, and other Poems*, *Empedocles on Ætna*, *Lectures on Translating Homer*, *Essays on Criticism*, *Merope*, and *Tristram and Iseult.* His subjects are drawn both from the classics and from the romances of his country. He is reputed one of the editors of *The Academy*, an English journal.

GEORGE WILLIAM CURTIS, 1824-——, is a native of Rhode Island. He began his career of authorship by producing the *Nile Notes of a Howadji*, written when he was travelling on the river Nile. This was followed by the *Howadji in Syria*, and *Lotus Eating*. Mr. Curtis was in 1852 one of the original editors of *Putnam's Monthly Magazine*, in the columns of which first appeared *The Potiphar Papers*, a caricature of fashionable life in New York city. Among his other writings are *Prue and I*, and *Trumps*. Mr. Curtis is a lecturer of finished eloquence, and discusses politics, literature, and the rights of woman. He is still a writer for the press, and the periodicals of Harper and Brothers contain many vigorous articles from his pen.

WILLIAM MORRIS, 1835-——, was born at Walthamstow, near London, and received the education of an English gentleman, graduating at Oxford. He early formed associations with a small knot of men in art and literature whose taste was cultivated by a profound study of historic art and of nature. In company with others he established a fine art business in London, which has done much to introduce a high order of decorative art, not only into ecclesiastical but into domestic architecture. Mr. Morris's best known poetical works are *The Life and Death of Jason*, and *The Earthly Paradise*, the latter a collection of stories, drawn half from classic, half from northern myths, told with exquisite grace and warmth of color. His style is remarkable for the skill with which he uses the best English words for his purpose, recovering many that have dropped out of use, and giving a quaint archaic touch to his writing. In a period when poetry is largely subjective in tone, he is preëminently a story-teller, dealing with form and color in his poetic art, and giving the appreciating reader almost the pleasure of looking at a picture; his men and women are heroes and heroines of a fair world, in which they move, not far from human sympathy, but just above human likeness. His studies have been largely in early Icelandic literature, and he has translated into prose some of the Sagas, in company with E. Magnussen, an Icelandic scholar, rendering the stories into an English dress that is remarkable for its antique form and the richness of its Saxon phrase. *The Story of Grettir the Strong*, and *The Story of the Volsungs and Niblungs*, belong to this class. Mr. Morris is to be associated in current English literature with the painter and poet Dante Gabriel Rossetti, and with Algernon Charles Swinburne, although the last named has shown an eagerness for sensual subjects, which is likely to destroy the interest felt in his singular melody of verse.

In these *First Steps* we have been obliged to neglect the loved and honored name of many an author of high rank, whose works we should have been delighted to study; but if we have obtained a comprehensive view of the subject, and have become sufficiently interested to continue the study further, the object presented at the outset is accomplished.

Though the present age exhibits a greater development of prose romance than of any other class of English literature, the writers of our generation have produced very much that is not prose, and much that is not romance. We have had Hallam, and Froude, and Motley; Brougham, De Quincey, and Arnold; Lowell, and Holmes, and Curtis; Longfellow, Tennyson, and Whittier; Carlyle, Ruskin, and Emerson; Wayland, Whately, and Hamilton; and we might mention many more, the fruit of whose thought is the strong meat upon which the manly American as well as the hearty children of Britain are to be nourished and strengthened for their progress onward and upward!

The first literary character we found in Britain was the bard or gleeman, who was a wanderer sometimes, but often appeared as a retainer of the baron, in whose lofty hall he recited the history or fable of older days. He was a favorite with the baron's hearth-sharers, and when the board was cleared, and the cup-bearers passed the foamy mead from guest to guest, he arose to sing of love and of war. Clad in his flowing robes, with his venerable beard, as he became more and more excited by his song, he transmitted his enthusiasm to the rough men about the board, and the hall was merry.

In the dimly lighted cloisters of the Benedictine Abbey the literary man of England was long buried. There, hidden from the world, he was permitted to labor lovingly, with more thought for the letter than for the spirit of the Gospel he so splendidly illuminated. There, walking under the round Norman arches, and up the steep stone stairway, we saw him at his work.

Next, when our speech was little used in books, we paid a visit to two of the Greyfriars, or Franciscans, and found Roger Bacon, and his master Robert Grosseteste, Bishop of Lincoln, dressed in their coarse gray gowns, with heads and feet bare. Belonging to an order the aim of which was to heal the poor and succor the distressed, they were explorers of nature and students of doctrine, and they gave scholarship a more practical direction.

In our next period we found that abuses had arisen in the land by reason of the mendicant friars, and the author of the *Vision of Piers Plowman*, in our earliest allegory, produced his charming pictures of life, and, with a love for the people, labored to give them the right to read the Bible, and fought every variety of abuse of power. John Wiclif too, issued from his quiet home at Lutterworth those stirring conversations and appeals which sent the English laymen and humble priests all over the land preaching the doctrines of the Lollards, and the supremacy of the Bible.

At this time that shadowy knight, Sir Thomas Malory, gave the land his collection of Round Table Romances, which in their disconnected form had already modified our literature, but which in their new arrangement have not yet ceased to exert their influence.

Then too, Chaucer and Gower and Latimer arose, all modified by the sturdy Lollard of Lutterworth.

The next chapter showed us the famous Mermaid Club, instituted by Sir Walter Raleigh, the favorite of Queen Elizabeth; and we were pleased with the wit-combats between Shakespeare and Jonson, of which old Thomas Fuller had imagined the details before us. We liked to think of these giants surrounded by Beaumont, Fletcher, Selden, Carew, Donne, and others, even if we were doubtful of the truth of the picture. It might have been true.

These all passed away. In the same Bread Street on which the Mermaid Inn was situated, John Milton, the ornament of the next period, was born. We saw him sitting in Whitehall, Latin secretary to Oliver Cromwell.

Cromwell died, and Charles II. came again to Whitehall, and it was the very year that John Bunyan entered the jail at Bedford. While Bunyan was working at his great allegory, Pepys and Evelyn were making those minute records of court life and political doings which are so charming as we read them to-day. The great wits were holding their historic meetings at Will's Coffee-House, and Addison and Steele were noting their doings. The comic dramatists were corrupting the theatres, and Dryden was debasing English verse.

The next chapter showed us the people captivated with Robinson Crusoe, devoutly singing the sweet lyrics of Watts, and exciting their baser passions with the pages of Smollett or Fielding.

It was a pleasanter scene, when we looked upon the Literary Club of Dr. Johnson, and saw a picture, which the painter's pencil and the graver's burin have reproduced, that we may hang it upon the walls of our homes and keep fresh in our memory the forms of the giants there were in those days.

Before we leave our literary friends, we must cast one glance at the turreted pile called Abbotsford, and drop a tear upon the grave of Scott under the ruined arches of Dryburgh Abbey. We must give one long wishful look at the Sleepy Hollow to which, in fulfillment of his early dreams, Washington Irving stole away from the world and its distractions, and, under the shades of his ivy-covered cottage at Sunnyside, dreamed away the last golden days of his fruitful life.

A CHART SHOWING THE HISTORY OF BIBLE TRANSLATIONS.

THE MANUSCRIPT BIBLE.

Reign	Date	Translation
Before the Conquest.		
A. D.	700?	The Psalms translated by Bishop Aldhelm.
	735.	The Gospel of St. John, by the Venerable Bede.
	880.	The Commandments, and parts of Exodus and the Psalms, by King Alfred, and by his orders.
	990?	Most of the Old Testament. Archb'p Ælfric.
		A Pause in the Work.
Edward III.	1327–1377.	
	1340.	The Psalms, by Richard Rolle, of Hampole.
		Another Pause.
Richard II.	1377–1399.	
	1380.	The New Testament, from the Latin Vulgate, by Wiclif.
	1382.	The Old Testament, from the Latin Vulgate, by Wiclif, or one of his friends.
	1388.	Revision of the above by John Purvey, widely circulated.

THE PRINTED BIBLE.

Reign	Date	Translation
Henry VIII.	1509–1547.	
	1525.	The New Testament, by William Tyndale. Printed at Cologne.
	1530.	The Pentateuch, by William Tyndale.
	1534.	The Book of Jonah, by William Tyndale.
	1534.	The New Testament, by George Joye. Printed at Antwerp.
	1535.	The New Testament, by William Tyndale.
	1535.	The Bible, by Miles Coverdale.
	1537.	The Bible, by "Thomas Matthews." J. Rogers.
	1538.	The New Testament, by Miles Coverdale. In Latin, revised.
	1539.	The "Great Bible," by Miles Coverdale.
	1539.	The Bible, by R. Taverner, a Greek scholar.
		Another Pause.
Mary.	1553–1558.	
	1557.	"Genevan" Bible begun. It was a quarto.
Elizabeth.	1558–1603.	
	1560.	"Genevan" Bible, completed. Became the Household Bible.
	1568.	The "Bishops'" Bible, finished by Archbishop Parker and others.
	1582.	The New Testament at Rheims, from the Vulgate.
		Another Pause.
James I.	1603–1625.	
	1609.	The Old Testament from the Vulgate. Published at Douay.
	1611.	The Authorized Version finished. (Begun in 1607.)

BIBLIOGRAPHY.

THE student who wishes to advance beyond the first steps in English Literature must make himself familiar with the authors in the best editions of their works. The following bibliographical list aims to include correct and available editions, avoiding such as are of excessive cost. Other things being equal, preference is given to American publications.

Some of the authors do not, however, appear either in American editions or in editions of low price. This is especially true of books of the period of immature English, which are not in great popular demand. A number of societies exist in England, organized for the purpose of republishing such of these works as have exerted an influence upon literature. Among these are The Roxburghe Club, The Early English Text Society, The Chaucer Society, The Ælfric Society, and The Camden, Shakespeare, and Percy Societies. These have done and are still doing a grand work in familiarizing our generation with much that merits remembrance, though their publications are in many instances quite expensive, and often very scarce. For the student they are indispensable, but the general reader may find some of the same works in cheaper and less scholarly forms. The English reprints, edited by Edward Arber, and published by Alexander Murray and Son, London, are elegant and cheap, and the well-known libraries of Henry G. Bohn, now published by Bell and Daldy, London, are too familiar to need description here. The Tauchnitz Editions, published in Leipzig, which include many authors mentioned in this book, are readily obtained. These are cheap and uniform. Some of the publications of John Russell Smith, of London, are also worthy of notice; and the "Clarendon Press Series" publishing by Macmillan & Co., London and New York, comprises works that are at once scholarly and cheap.

ADDISON, JOSEPH, — Complete. By *Prof. G. W. Greene.* 6 vols. 12mo, 1853. Philadelphia, J. B. Lippincott & Co.
Complete, 3 vols. 8vo. New York, Harper & Bros.
Spectator, *A. Chalmers.* 8 vols. 16mo. Boston, Little, Brown, & Co.
Spectator in Miniature. 2 vols. 18mo. New York, Harper & Bros.

ÆLFRIC'S HOMILIES. — Translated by *Benjamin Thorpe.* London, Ælfric Society, 2 vols. 8vo, 1843, 1846.

ALFRED THE GREAT. — *Jubilee Edition*, whole works, with preliminary essays. 2 vols. 8vo. London, 1858. *Rev. Samuel Fox.* Boethius's Consolation of Philosophy Bohn's Antiquarian Library. London, Bell & Daldy.

ANCREN RIWLE, THE: A treatise on the rules and duties of monastic life, edited and translated by *James Morton, B A.* London, 1853. Small quarto. Camden Society.

ARNOLD, MATTHEW. — Essays in Criticism, 1 vol. 16mo; and New Poems, 1 vol. 16mo. Boston, Fields, Osgood, & Co

ARNOLD, THOMAS. — Lectures on Modern History, 1 vol. 12mo; and History of Rome, 1 vol. 8vo. New York, D. Appleton & Co.

Life and Correspondence, by *Arthur Penrhyn Stanley*. 2 vols. 12mo. Boston, Fields, Osgood, & Co.

ASCHAM, ROGER. — Complete Works, by *Rev. Dr. Giles*, 4 vols. 8vo. London, John Russell Smith, 1866.

Toxophilus and the Schoolmaster, by *Edward Arber*. 2 vols. London, A. Murray & Son.

BACON, FRANCIS. — Most complete edition. By *J. Spedding*, *R. L. Ellis*, and *D. D. Heath*. 15 vols. 8vo. New York, Hurd & Houghton.

Essays, Annotated by *Archbishop Whately*, with glossarial index. 1 vol. 8vo. Boston, Lee & Shepard, 1869.

Novum Organum and Advancement of Learning. Bohn's Scientific Library. 1 vol. 12mo. Bell & Daldy, London, 1868.

BACON, ROGER. — *Opus Majus*, edited by Dr. Samuel Jebb. 1 vol. folio. London, 1733.

BAXTER, RICHARD. — Works, with Preface, Memoir, and Essay on his Life and Genius. 4 vols. 8vo. London, 1854. Little, Brown, & Co., Boston.

Reformed Pastor. 1 vol. 8vo. R. Carter & Bros., New York.

BEAUMONT AND FLETCHER. — A popular selection by *Leigh Hunt*. 1 vol. 12mo. Bohn's Standard Library.

BENTHAM, JEREMY. — Works, by *Sir J. Bowring*. 11 vols. 8vo. Edinburgh, 1843.

BEOWULF. — *John M. Kemble*. 12mo. London, 1833. This edition contains a glossary.

A. D. Wackerbarth. 16mo. London, 1849. In English verse.

Best edition by *Benjamin Thorpe*, published in England. Expensive and difficult to be obtained in this country.

BERKELEY, BISHOP GEORGE. — Works and Life. *J. Stock*. London, 1820. 3 vols. 8vo.

BIBLE, THE, Versions of. — *Bosworth and Waring*. Four versions of A. D. 360, 995, 1389 (Wiclif), and 1586 (Tindale). 1 vol. 8vo. London, J. Russell Smith.

Annals of the English Bible, by C. Anderson. 2 vols. 8vo. London, 1845.

BOLINGBROKE, LORD. — Works, edited by David Mallet. 5 vols. 4to. London, 1754.

BROUGHAM, HENRY, LORD. — Speeches. 4 vols. 8vo. 1843.
Historical Sketches of Statesmen and Men of Letters and Science of the Time of George III. 3 vols. 8vo. 1843.

BROWNE, WILLIAM.—Life and Poems. Chalmers's English Poets, vol. vi.

BROWNING, ELIZABETH BARRETT. — Complete Works. 5 vols. 32mo. New York, James Miller.

BROWNING, ROBERT. — Complete Works. 7 vols. 16mo. Boston, Fields, Osgood, & Co.

BRYANT, WILLIAM CULLEN. — Poetical Works. 3 vols. 12mo New York, D. Appleton & Co.
Letters. 2 vols. 12mo. New York, G. P. Putnam & Son.
Translation of the Iliad of Homer. 2 vols. 8vo. Boston, Fields, Osgood, & Co.

BUNYAN, JOHN. — Works, with preface by *George Whitefield.* 2 vols. folio. London, 1767–68.
Pilgrim's Progress, with Notes by G. Offor, 110 illustrations, engraved by Dalziels. 1 vol. quarto. New York, G. Routledge & Sons.
Illustrated Edition. 8vo. New York, American Tract Society.
Illustrated Edition. 24mo. Philadelphia, J. B. Lippincott & Co.
Illustrated Edition. 32mo. Notes by *Newton, Bradford,* and *Hawkes.* New York, G. Routledge & Sons.
Illustrated. By *Southey,* 1 vol. 12mo. New York, Harper & Bros.

BURKE, EDMUND. — Complete Works. 12 vols. crown 8vo. Boston, Little, Brown, & Co.
Complete Works. Bohn's British Classics. 9 vols. 12mo. London, Bell & Daldy.
Works, with a Memoir. 3 vols. 8vo. New York, Harper & Bros.

BURNET, GILBERT. — History of My Own Time, with Notes by *Dartmouth, Hardwicke, Onslow,* and *Swift;* and History of the Reformation of the Church of England. 3 vols. 8vo. London, 1857. Little, Brown, & Co., Boston.

BURNS, ROBERT. — Life and Works, by *Robert Chambers.* 4 vols. 12mo. New York, Harper & Bros.
Globe Edition. 1 vol. crown 8vo. McMillan & Co., London. The best cheap and complete.
Poems. 3 vols. 18mo. Boston, Fields, Osgood, & Co.
Poems, with Glossary, etc. 1 vol. 12mo. New York D. Appleton & Co.
Poems, 1 vol. Tauchnitz Edition. New York, Leypoldt & Holt.

BUTLER, SAMUEL. — Poems and Life, in Chalmers' English Poets, vol. viii.

Poems, edited by *Rev. George Gilfillan.* 2 vols. in 1. 8vo. New York, 1858.

Hudibras, with Notes by *Nash.* 1 vol. 16mo. Globe Edition. New York, D. Appleton & Co.

Hudibras, with Life of Butler. 1 vol. 32mo. Boston, Roberts Bros.

Complete Poems. 2 vols. 18mo. Fields, Osgood, & Co., Boston.

BYRON, LORD. — Poems. 10 vols. 18mo. Boston, Fields, Osgood, & Co.

Complete Works, with Life by Moore. 4 vols. 8vo. New York, W. J. Widdleton.

Tauchnitz Edition. 5 vols. New York, Leypoldt & Holt.

CÆDMON. — *Wm. H. F. Bosanquet,* translated into English verse. London, 1860.

CAMPBELL, THOMAS. — Poems. 1 vol. 18mo. Boston, Fields, Osgood, & Co.

Poems. 1 vol. 12mo. New York, D. Appleton & Co.

CARLYLE, THOMAS. — Works. 6 vols. 12mo. New York, Harper & Bros.

Critical and Miscellaneous Essays. 4 vols. 8vo. New York, Hurd & Houghton.

Best edition now publishing, by Chapman & Hall, London, and Scribner, Welford, & Co., New York. To be in about 30 vols. 8vo. Revised by the author.

Tauchnitz Edition. 20 vols. New York, Leypoldt & Holt.

CHAUCER, GEOFFREY. — By *Alexander Chalmers,* in his English Poets, vol. i. 8vo. London, 1810.

Canterbury Tales, by *Thomas Tyrwhitt,* with Essay and Notes, London, 1822. 5 vols. 12mo.

Prologue to the Canterbury Tales; The Knightes Tale; The Nonne Prestes Tale. 1 vol. Macmillan & Co.

Legende of Goode Women, by *Hiram Corson,* with Notes, etc. 1 vol. 8vo. Leypoldt & Holt, New York.

The Early English Text Society has published Chaucer's Prose Works in several volumes by various editors.

CHEKE, SIR JOHN. — See *Chalmers'* Biographical Dictionary vol. ix. p. 225.

CHRONICLE, THE ANGLO-SAXON. — Edited by *Benjamin Thorpe.* 2 vols. London, 1861.

COLERIDGE, SAMUEL TAYLOR. — Complete in 7 vols. 8vo. By *Rev. W. G. T. Shedd, D. D.,* with a valuable introductory essay and notes. New York, Harper & Bros.

Poems. 1 vol. Tauchnitz Edition. New York, Leypoldt & Holt.

COLLIER, JEREMY. — A Short View of the Immorality and Profaneness of the English Stage. London. 1 vol. 8vo. 1698.

COLLINS, WILLIAM. — Poems. 1 volume 18mo. Boston, Fields, Osgood, & Co.

CONGREVE, WILLIAM. — *Chalmers's* English Poets, vol. x.

COOPER, JAMES FENIMORE. — Works, with a biographical sketch by *Wm. Cullen Bryant.* 32 vols. 8vo. New York, Hurd & Houghton.

COVERDALE, MILES. — Writings and Translations, by *G. Pearson.* Parker Society, Cambridge, 1844 8vo.

COWLEY, ABRAHAM. — Life and Works, in *Chalmers's* English Poets, vol. vii.

Essays, with Life, Notes, and Illustrations. 1 vol. 18mo. Boston, Roberts Bros.

COWPER, WILLIAM.—Complete Works, by *Southey*, illustrated. 8 vols. In Bohn's Library, London, Bell & Daldy.

Poems, by *Rev. Thos. Dale.* 2 vols. 8vo. New York, Harper & Bros.

Poems. 3 vols. 18mo. Boston, Fields, Osgood, & Co.

CRABBE, REV. GEORGE. — Poems, with those of Heber and Pollock. 1 vol. 8vo. Philadelphia, J. B. Lippincott & Co.

CRANMER, BISHOP THOMAS. — By *J. E. Cox.* 2 vols. 8vo. Parker Society, Cambridge, 1844–46.

CUDWORTH, RALPH. — Intellectual System, Immutable Morality, etc. 2 vols. 8vo. Andover, 1837–38.

CURTIS, GEORGE WILLIAM. — Works. 6 vols. 12mo. New York, Harper & Bros.

DAVENANT, SIR WILLIAM. — Works. 2 vols. in 1, folio. London, 1673. (Is in American public libraries.)

Life and Poems. *Chalmers's* English Poets, vol. vi.

DEFOE, DANIEL. — Complete Works. By *Sir Walter Scott.* 7 vols. 8vo. Bohn's Library, Bell & Daldy, London.

Robinson Crusoe, various editions by Geo. Routledge & Sons, New York.

Robinson Crusoe. Illustrated. 1 vol. 8vo. Hurd & Houghton, New York.

Robinson Crusoe. 1 vol. Tauchnitz Edition. New York, Leypoldt & Holt.

DE QUINCEY, THOMAS. — Works. 22 vols. 16mo. Boston, Fields, Osgood, & Co.

DICKENS, CHARLES. — Riverside Edition, most complete American edition. 27 vols. crown 8vo. Illustrated. New York, Hurd & Houghton. $2 a volume.

Charles Dickens' edition. 14 vols. 16mo. Boston, Fields, Osgood, & Co.

Cheap edition. 17 vols. 8vo. New York, D. Appleton & Co.

DONNE, JOHN. — Works and Life, by *Henry Alford.* 6 vols. 8vo. London, 1839.

Also *Chalmers's* English Poets, vol. v.

DRAYTON, MICHAEL. — *Alexander Chalmers* in the Works of the English Poets from Chaucer to Cowper, vol. iv. 8vo. London, 1810.

DRUMMOND, WILLIAM OF HAWTHORNDEN.—Life and Poems. *Chalmers's* English Poets, vol. vi.

Poems, with portrait. *W. B. Turnbull.* J. Russell Smith. 1 vol. 16mo. London, 1856.

DRYDEN, JOHN. — Complete Works. Life by *Rev. John Mitford.* 2 vols. 8vo. New York, Harper & Bros.

Select Poems, edited by *W. D. Christie, M. A.* Clarendon Press Series. Macmillan & Co.

Poems. 5 vols. 18mo. Boston, Fields, Osgood, & Co.

Poems. 1 vol. 8vo. G. Routledge & Sons, New York.

Poems. 1 vol. 16mo. D. Appleton & Co., New York.

DWIGHT, TIMOTHY. —Theology explained and defended, in a series of sermons. 4 vols. 8vo. New York, Harper & Bros.

EDWARDS, JONATHAN. — Works. 4 vols. New York, R. Carter & Bros.

On the Will. 1 vol. Same publishers.

EMERSON, RALPH WALDO. — Essays and Poems. 11 vols. Boston, Fields, Osgood, & Co.

ETHERIDGE, SIR GEORGE. — Works containing his Plays and Poems. 1 vol. 12mo. London, 1704.

EVELYN, JOHN. — Diary and Correspondence, by *John Forster* Bohn's Library. Bell & Daldy, London.

FIELDING, HENRY. — Novels. Amelia, Tom Jones, Memoir by *Thos. Roscoe.* 3 vols. 12mo. New York, Harper & Bros.

Selected Novels, with Smollett's. 6 vols. New York, G. Routledge & Sons.

Tom Jones, 1 vol. Tauchnitz edition. New York, Leypoldt & Holt.

FORD, JOHN. — An expurgated edition in *Murray's* Family Library. London, 1847.

Best edition, edited by Gifford. 2 vols. 8vo. London, 1827.

FRANKLIN, BENJAMIN. — Works, by *Jared Sparks.* 10 vols. 8vo. B ston, 1840. New edition, Philadelphia, 1858.

Autobiography, by *Hon. John Bigelow.* 1 vol. 12mo. Philadelphia.

FROUDE, JAMES ANTHONY. — History of England, 12 vols. 8vo, and Short Studies, 1 vol. 8vo. New York, Charles Scribner & Co.

FULLER, THOMAS. — Church History of Britain. *J. Nichols.* 3 vols. 8vo. London, 1842.

Worthies of England. *P. A. Nuttall.* 3 vols. 8vo. London, 1840.

Holy and Profane State. 1 vol. 16mo. London, 1840. Also 1 vol. 16mo. Boston, Little, Brown, & Co.

Good Thoughts in Bad Times, and other Papers. 1 vol. 16mo. Boston, Fields, Osgood, & Co.

GAY, JOHN. — Poems. 2 vols. 18mo. Boston, Fields, Osgood & Co.

GIBBON, EDWARD. — Decline and Fall of the Roman Empire, with Notes by *Milman* and *Guizot.* 6 vols. 12mo. New York, Harper & Bros.

GOLDSMITH, OLIVER. — Miscellaneous Works, by *James Prior.* 4 vols. 12mo. G. P. Putnam & Son, New York.

Life, by *Washington Irving,* 2 vols.; History of Greece, 1 vol.; History of Rome, edited by *H. W. Herbert,* 1 vol.; Vicar of Wakefield, 1 vol.; all 18mo; and Poetical Works, edited by *Bolton Corney,* 1 vol. 8vo., New York, Harper & Bros.

Select Works. 1 vol. with portrait. Tauchnitz edition. New York, Leypoldt & Holt.

GOWER, JOHN. — Confessio Amantis, with life. *Alexander Chalmers,* English Poets, vol. ii. London, 1810.

By *Dr. Reinbold Pauli,* with a glossary and life. 3 vols. 8vo. London, 1857.

GRAY, THOMAS. — Poems. 1 vol. 18mo. Boston, Fields, Osgood, & Co.

Poems. 1 vol. 32mo. New York, James Miller.

GROSSETESTE, ROBERT. — By *M. Cooke.* Chasteau d'Amour, and other Works. 8vo. London, Caxton Society. J. Russell Smith.

HALLAM, HENRY. — Constitutional History, — Middle Ages, — and Literature of Europe. 3 vols. 8vo. Boston, 1865.

Same in 4 vols. 8vo. New York, Harper & Bros.

Best edition. 10 vols. crown 8vo. New York, W. J. Widdleton.

HAMILTON, SIR WILLIAM. — Discussions on Philosophy, Literature, Education, and University Reform, by *Rev. Robert Turnbull.* 1 vol. 8vo. Harper & Bros., New York.

HAWTHORNE, NATHANIEL. — Works. Complete edition. 17 vols. 16mo. Fields, Osgood, & Co., Boston.

HERBERT, GEORGE. — British Poets. 1 vol. 18mo. Boston, Fields, Osgood, & Co.
Globe Edition. 1 vol. 16mo. New York, D. Appleton & Co.
Works. 2 vols. 8vo. London, 1846.
HOLMES, OLIVER WENDELL. — Poetical Works, complete. 1 vol. 16mo, and other editions. Boston, Fields, Osgood, & Co.
HOOD, THOMAS. — Complete Works. 6 vols. 8vo. New York, G. P. Putnam & Son.
HOOKER, REV. RICHARD. — Works, by *Rev. John Keble.* 3 vols. Oxford, 1845.
HOPKINS, MARK. — Lectures on Moral Science. 1 vol. 12mo. Boston, Gould & Lincoln.
Law of Love and Love as a Law. 1 vol. crown 8vo. New York, C. Scribner & Co.
HUME, DAVID. — History of England, with a sketch of the author's life. 6 vols. 12mo. New York, Harper & Bros.
Same, Boston, 1868.
Philosophical Works. 4 vols. 8vo. Boston, 1854.
HUNT, J. H. LEIGH. — Autobiography. 2 vols. 12mo. Men, Women, and Books. 2 vols. 12mo. The Foster Brother. 1 volume, 8vo. New York, Harper & Bros.
A Book for a Corner. 1 vol. 12mo. London.
A Day by the Fire. 1 vol. Boston, Roberts Bros.
The Book of the Sonnet, a posthumous work. 2 vols. post 8vo. Boston, Roberts Bros.

IRVING, WASHINGTON. — Complete Works. Sunnyside edition. 28 vols. 12mo. People's edition, 26 vols. 16mo. Also other editions published by G. P. Putnam & Son, New York.

JOHNSON, SAMUEL. — Works, with an Essay on his Life and Genius, by *Arthur Murphy.* 2 vols. 8vo. New York, Harper & Bros.
History of Rasselas. 1 vol. 32mo. New York, D. Appleton & Co.
Life by Boswell, Notes by Crocker. 2 vols. 8vo. New York, Harper & Bros.
Same, 4 vols. 12mo, profusely illustrated. New York, Geo. Routledge & Sons.
Same, Globe edition, 1 vol. New York, Geo. Routledge & Sons.
Lives of the Poets. 2 vols. Tauchnitz edition. New York, Leypoldt & Holt.
JONSON, BEN. — Works, with Notes and Memoir, by *W. Gifford.* 9 vols. 8vo. Moxon, London, 1855.

KEBLE, JOHN.—The Christian Year. 1 vol. 16mo Boston, E. P. Dutton & Co.
Life by J. T. Coleridge. 2 vols. crown 8vo. London, 1869.
KNOX, JOHN.—Life by *T. M'Crie*. 2 vols. 8vo. Edinburgh, 1813.
Complete Works, by *David Laing*, Edinburgh.

LAMB, CHARLES.—Complete Works. 5 vols. crown 8vo. New York, W. J. Widdleton.
Complete Works, by *T. Noon Talfourd*. 2 vols. 12mo. New York, Harper & Bros.
LATIMER, BISHOP HUGH.—By *G. E. Corrie*. 2 vols. 8vo. Parker Society, Cambridge, Eng., 1844–45.
By *Edward Arber*. Sermon on the Ploughers, and Seven Sermons before Edward VI. 2 vols. fac-simile. London, A. Murray & Son.
LANDOR, WALTER SAVAGE.—Works complete. 2 vols. 8vo. London, 1868.
Selections, by *G. S. Hillard*. 1 vol. 8vo. Boston, 1856.
LAYAMON'S BRUT, or Chronicle of Britain. By *Sir Frederic Madden*, Keeper of the MSS. in the British Museum. 3 vols. London, Society of Antiquaries, 1847.
LOCKE, JOHN.—Complete edition. Life by *Lord King*. 11 vols. 8vo. London, 1824–30. Boston, Little, Brown, & Co.
Thoughts on Education. Essay on Study and Reading. 2 vols. 32mo. New York, J. W. Schemmerhorn, 1869.
Philosophical Works, by *J. A. St. John*, and Life, Letters, etc., by *Lord King*, 3 vols. in Bohn's Standard Library, Bell & Daldy, London.
LONGFELLOW, HENRY WADSWORTH.—Complete Works. 4 vols. 16mo. Boston, Fields, Osgood, & Co.
Translation of Dante. 3 vols. royal 8vo. Same Publishers.
LOWELL, J. RUSSELL.—Poetical Works, complete. 2 vols. 16mo. Boston, Fields, Osgood, & Co.
Fireside Travels. 1 vol. 16mo.
Biglow Papers. 2 vols. 16mo.
Vision of Sir Launfal. 1 vol. 16mo.
Under the Willows. 1 vol. 16mo.
Among my Books. 1 vol.
The Cathedral. 1 vol.
LYLY, JOHN.—Dramatic Works, by *F. W. Fairholt*. London, 1858. 2 vols. 8vo.
Euphues, and Euphues and his England, by *Edward Arber*, from the editions of 1579–80. 1 vol. London, Alex Murray & Son

LYTTON, EDWARD BULWER, LORD. — Novels. Globe Edition, 22 vols. 16mo. Philadelphia, J. B. Lippincott & Co.

Novels in over 40 vols. Tauchnitz edition. New York, Leypoldt & Holt.

Dramas and Poems, with steel portrait. 1 vol. 32mo. Boston, Roberts, Bros.

MALORY, SIR THOMAS. — La Morte d'Arthur. Edited by *Thomas Wright*. 3 vols. 8vo. London, 1866. John Russell Smith.

MANDEVILLE, SIR JOHN. — *Thomas Wright*, in Bohn's Antiquarian Library. Early Travels in Palestine. 1 vol. 12mo. London, 1848.

MANNYNGE, ROBERT OF BRUNNE. Edited by *Frederick J. Furnivall, M. A.* London, 1862, printed by the Roxburghe Club.

MARLOWE, CHRISTOPHER. — Old English Plays, by *R. Dodsley*, London, 1825–27. Vol. ii. Edward II.; vol. viii. The Jew of Malta.

MILTON, JOHN. — Works and Life. *Rev. John Milford.* 8 vols. 8vo. Pickering, London, 1851. Costly.

Prose Works complete. By *Dr. Sumner*, Bishop of Winchester. Bohn's Standard Library. 5 vols. 8vo. Bell & Daldy, London, 1852.

Poems. Clarendon Press Series, 2 vols. 8vo.

Paradise Lost, edited with Notes under direction of Prof. Torrey of Harvard. 1 vol. 16mo. New York, Hurd & Houghton.

Complete Poetical Works. 1 vol. 16mo. New York, D. Appleton & Co.

Poetical Works. Household Edition. Illustrated. Geo. Routledge & Co., London and New York.

MONTAGUE, LADY. — Letters and Works, edited by *Lord Wharncliffe.* 3 vols. 8vo. London, 1837.

Letters, with a Life by *Sarah Jane Hale*. 1 vol. 12mo. Boston, Roberts Bros.

MOORE, THOMAS. — Poetical Works. 1 vol. 8vo. New York, Geo. Routledge & Sons.

Poems. 6 vols. 18mo. Boston, Fields, Osgood, & Co.

Life of Byron. 2 vols. 8vo. New York, Harper & Bros.

Lalla Rookh. 1 vol. 8vo., with notes and illustrations. New York, Hurd & Houghton.

Same. Cheap edition. 1 vol. 32mo. New York, D. Appleton & Co.

MORE, SIR THOMAS. — Lives of Edward V. and Richard III. In *W. Kennet's* History of England, vol. i. London, 1719.

Utopia, translated by Bishop Burnet.

Utopia. Reprinted in fac-simile from the editions of 1551 and 1556, edited by *Edward Arber*, and published by A. Murray & Son, London, 1868. Cheap and excellent.

Best edition of Utopia, edited by *J. A. St. John.* 1 vol. 12mo. London, 1845.

MORRIS, WILLIAM.—Life and Death of Jason. 1 vol. 16mo. Boston, Roberts Bros.

The Earthly Paradise. 2 vols. crown 8vo. Boston, Roberts Bros.

MOTLEY, JOHN LOTHROP.—Dutch Republic. 3 vols. 8vo New York, Harper & Bros.

United Netherlands. 4 vols. 8vo. New York, Harper & Bros

NEWTON, SIR ISAAC.—Life by *Sir David Brewster.* New York, 1831. Later edition, very much enlarged. 2 vols. 8vo. London, 1855.

Complete Works, edited by *Bishop Horsley.* 5 vols. 4to. 1779–85.

Principia, edited by *Brougham* and *E. J. Routh*, 1855. Best edition.

ORMULUM, THE.—By *Robert Meadows White, D. D.* 2 vols. 8vo. Oxford, 1852.

OTWAY, THOMAS.—Poems and Life. *Chalmers's* English Poets, vol. viii.

PECOCKE, BISHOP REGINALD.—By *Churchill Babington.* 2 vols. London, 1860.

PEPYS, SAMUEL.—Diary and Correspondence, by *Lord Braybrooke.* Bohn's Library. 4 vols. London, Bell & Daldy.

PERCY, BISHOP THOMAS.—Reliques of Ancient English Poetry. 1 vol. 8vo. Geo. Routledge & Sons, New York.

Reliques. 3 vols. Tauchnitz edition. New York, Leypoldt & Holt.

PIERS PLOWMAN.—By *Rev. W. W. Skeat, M. A.* Published by Macmillan & Co., London and New York. 1 vol. 8vo. This is the best edition for general readers.

By *Rev. W. W. Skeat.* Early English Text Society. 3 large vols. London. The best edited edition. Expensive.

POE, EDGAR ALLAN.—Complete Works. 4 vols. 8vo. New York, W. J. Widdleton.

POPE, ALEXANDER.—Life by *Robert Carruthers;* Iliad, notes by *Watson;* Odyssey, with Flaxman's illustrations. 4 vols. 12mo. In Bohn's Illustrated Library. Bell & Daldy, London.

Poems. 3 vols. 18mo. Boston, Fields, Osgood, & Co.
Globe Edition. 1 vol. 16mo. New York, D. Appleton & Co.

PRESCOTT, WILLIAM HICKLING. — Works. 15 vols. 8vo. Philadelphia, J. B. Lippincott & Co.

QUARLES, FRANCIS.
Enchiridion, London, published by J. Russell Smith, 1 vol. 16mo. 1856.
Boanerges and Barnabas, edited by *Rev. F. H. Brett.* 1 vol. 12mo. London, 1855.

RAMSAY, ALLAN. — Complete edition, with biography by *Geo. Chalmers*, and Glossary. 2 vols. 8vo. London, 1800.
Gentle Shepherd, New York, 1854.

RICHARDSON, SAMUEL. — With prefatory memoir by *Sir Walter Scott*, in Ballantyne's Novelists' Library. London, 1821–24. Vols. vi., vii., viii.
Clarissa Harlowe. 4 vols. Tauchnitz edition. New York, Leypoldt & Holt.

ROBERTSON, WILLIAM. — Works edited by *John Frost.* 3 vols. 8vo. New York, Harper & Bros.

ROGERS, SAMUEL. — Poems and Italy. Richly illustrated. 2 vols. 8vo. London, 1854.
Poetical Works, 128 steel engravings. 4to. New York, Geo. Routledge & Sons.
Pleasures of Memory. 1 vol. 12mo. London.

RUSKIN, JOHN. — Complete Works. 14 vols. 12mo. New York, John Wiley & Son, 1867.

SCOTT, SIR WALTER. — Illustrated Library Edition. 25 vols. 16mo. Boston, Fields, Osgood, & Co. An excellent edition.
Waverley Novels. Library Edition. 25 vols. 8vo Edinburgh, 1852.
Same. 48 vols. 8vo. Philadelphia, J. B. Lippincott & Co.
People's Edition. Same publishers, 6 vols. 8vo.
Poetical Works. Globe Edition. Same publishers. 1 vol. 12mo.
Poems. 9 vols. 18mo. Boston, Fields, Osgood, & Co.
Waverley Novels. Cheap edition. 25 vols. fine type. New York, D. Appleton & Co.

SELDEN, JOHN. — Table Talk, by *S. W. Singer.* London, 1860.
Same, by *Edward Arber*, from the edition of 1689. London, Alex. Murray & Son, 1868.

SHAKESPEARE, WILLIAM. — For the thorough student. Complete Works, carefully edited by *Richard Grant White.* 12 vols. 8vo. Boston, Little, Brown, & Co., 1866.

For the general reader. Complete Works, edited by *Charles Knight,* with 1200 illustrations. 8 vols. 8vo. London, 1866.

Select Plays, in the Clarendon Press Series. Macmillan & Co., London and New York.

SHELLY, PERCY BYSSHE.—Poems. 4 vols. 18mo. Boston, Fields, Osgood, & Co.

SIDNEY, SIR PHILIP. — Complete Works. 3 vols. 8vo. London, 1725.

Miscellaneous Works, with Memoir, by *W. Gray.* Oxford, 1829, Boston, 1860.

Arcadia, edited by *Hain Friswell.* 8vo. London, 1867.

Apology for Poetry, by *Edward Arber.* London, A. Murray & Son, 1 vol. Reprint from edition of London, 1595.

SKELTON, JOHN. — By *Rev. Alexander Dyce.* 2 vols. 8vo. London, Rodd, 1843.

SMITH, ADAM. — Wealth of Nations, by *McCulloch.* Best edition. 4 vols. 8vo. Edinburgh, 1828.

Cheap Edition. 8vo. Edinburgh, 1863. Both to be had of Little, Brown, & Co., Boston.

SMITH, SYDNEY. — Life and Letters. By *Lady Holland.* 2 vols. 12mo, and —

Moral Philosophy. 1 vol. 12mo. Both published by Harper & Bros., New York.

Wit and Wisdom, by *E. A. Duyckinck.* 1 vol. 8vo. New York, G P. Putnam & Son.

SMOLLETT, TOBIAS GEORGE. — Works, by *Thomas Roscoe,* illustrated. 1 vol. 8vo. London, 1863.

Humphry Clinker and Roderick Random. 2 vols. 12mo. with Roscoe's Memoir. New York, Harper & Bros.

Same Novels, 2 vols. Tauchnitz edition. New York, Leypoldt & Holt.

SOUTH, ROBERT. — Sermons. Library of Old English Divines, vols. i.–v. 8vo. New York, Hurd & Houghton.

SOUTHEY, ROBERT. — Life and Works, by his son, *Rev. C. C. Southey.* 1 vol. 8vo. New York, Harper & Bros.

The Doctor. 1 vol. 12mo. Same publishers.

Life of Nelson. 1 vol. 18mo. Same publishers.

Life of John Wesley. 2 vols. 12mo. Same publishers.

Commonplace Book. 2 vols. 8vo. Same publishers.

Poems. 10 vols. 18mo. Boston, Fields, Osgood, & Co.

SPENSER, EDMUND. — Poems and Life. *Chalmers's* English Poets, vol. iii.

Poems, with critical introduction, by *Geo. S. Hillard.* **5 vols.** Boston, 1839.

Poems with Notes. 5 vols. Boston, Little, Brown, & Co.

Faerie Queene. 1 vol. 8vo. Clarendon Press Series. Macmillan & Co.

STEELE, SIR RICHARD. — The Tatler, 4 vols., and The Guardian, 3 vols. 16mo. Boston, Little, Brown, & Co.

English Humorists. *Thackeray.* 16mo. Philadelphia, J. B. Lippincott & Co. Also 12mo, 1 vol., Harper & Bros., New York.

STERNE, LAURENCE. — Works. 1 vol. 8vo. New York, Geo. Routledge & Sons.

Complete Works, with Life. 2 vols. 12mo. Philadelphia, J. B. Lippincott & Co.

Tristram Shandy, and Sentimental Journey. 2 vols. Tauchnitz edition. New York, Leypoldt & Holt.

STOWE, HARRIET BEECHER. — Complete Works. 12 vols. 12mo and 16mo. Boston, Fields, Osgood, & Co.

SWIFT, JONATHAN. — Poems. 3 vols. 18mo. Boston, Fields, Osgood, & Co.

Complete Works. By *Sir Walter Scott.* 19 vols. 8vo. Edinburgh, 1824.

Gulliver's Travels, with Life of Swift. 1 vol. 8vo. London, 1864. Boston, Little, Brown, & Co.

Gulliver's Travels. 1 vol. 12mo. Philadelphia, J. B. Lippincott & Co.

Gulliver's Travels. 1 vol. Tauchnitz edition. New York, Leypoldt & Holt.

TAYLOR, JEREMY. — Works and Life. *Reginald Heber.* 10 vols. 8vo. London, 1850–55.

Holy Living and Dying. *Ezra Abbot.* 2 vols. 12mo. Boston, Little, Brown, & Co., 1864.

Sermons, 1 vol. 8vo; and Life of Christ, 2 vols. 12mo. New York, R. Carter & Bros.

Life of Christ, with Life of Taylor, by *Rev. T. A. Buckley, M. A.* 1 vol. 8vo. New York, Geo. Routledge & Sons.

TENNYSON, ALFRED. — Poems complete. Farringford edition, 2 vols., and a variety of other editions. Boston, Fields, Osgood, & Co.

THACKERAY, WILLIAM MAKEPEACE. — Best edition. 22 vols. 8vo. London, Smith, Elder, & Co. 1870.

Household Edition. 6 vols. Ballads, 1 vol. 16mo. Early and Late Papers, 1 vol. 16mo. Boston, Fields, Osgood, & Co.

Thackeray's Novels are also published in cheap and attractive forms by Harper & Bros., New York.

THOMSON, JAMES. — Works. 4 vols. 12mo. London, 1762.
Seasons, illustrated. 1 vol. 8vo. New York, Harper & Bros.
Poems. 2 vols. 18mo. Boston, Fields, Osgood, & Co.

UDALL, NICHOLAS. — By *Edward Arber,* Ralph Royster Doyster from the unique copy at Eton College. A. Murray & Son, London.

VANBRUGH, SIR JOHN. — In *Cumberland's* British Drama, London, 1817, vols. 3 and 6.
The Comic Dramatists of the Restoration. By *Leigh Hunt* 8vo. London, 1840.

WALLER, EDMUND. — Life and Works, in *Chalmers's* English Poets, vol. viii.
WATTS, ISAAC. — Divine and Moral Songs. Illustrated. 1 vol. 4to. New York, Hurd & Houghton.
WAYLAND, FRANCIS. — Elements of Moral Science. New York, 1835.
WEBSTER, DANIEL. — Life and Works. By *Hon. Edward Everett.* 6 vols. 8vo. Boston, Little, Brown, & Co.
Private Correspondence and Autobiography. By his son, *Fletcher Webster.* 2 vols. 8vo. Same publishers.
WHATELY, RICHARD. — Elements of Logic. 1 vol. 12mo. New York, Sheldon & Co.
Elements of Rhetoric. 1 vol. 18mo. New York, Harper & Bros.
Kingdom of Christ. 1 vol. New York, R. Carter & Bros.
WHITTIER, JOHN GREENLEAF. — Prose Works complete, 2 vols. 16mo; and Poetical Works, complete diamond edition, 1 vol. Boston, Fields, Osgood, & Co.
WICLIF, JOHN. — Tracts and Treatises, with Memoir by *R. Vaughan.* 1 vol. 8vo. London, 1845.
WITHER, GEORGE. — Hymns, Songs, and Moral Odes. By *Edward Farr.* 1 vol. 12mo.; also —
Hymns and Songs of the Church. 1 vol. 16mo. James Russell Smith, London, 1856–57.
WORDSWORTH, WILLIAM. — Poetical Works. 8 vols. 8vo. Moxon, London.
Poems. 7 vols. 18mo. Boston, Fields, Osgood, & Co.
Poems. 2 vols. Tauchnitz edition. New York, Leypoldt & Holt.
WYCHERLEY, WILLIAM. — Plays. 1 vol. 16mo. London, 1842. Boston, Little, Brown, & Co.
Plays. Edited by *Leigh Hunt.* Moxon's edition. London.

EXPLANATIONS OF TITLES, PRONUNCIATION, ETC.

Aix, āks.
Ancren Riwle, ăn-krĕn′ ri-ūle.
Angeln, ăn′gĕln.
Arcadia, a pastoral district in Greece.
Aryan languages are those of which Sanscrit exhibits most nearly the original form. Aryan is derived from the Sanscrit, and means noble, and is kept in memory by the modern name Irán, for Persia.
Ascham, ăs′kăm.
Aurich, ow′rĭk.

Bede, beed.
Beowulf, be-o′woolf.
Biathanatos, death by violence.
Boccacio, bok-kät′chō.
Boethius, bo-ē′thi-us.
Bürger, būr′ger.

Cædmon, kăd′mon.
Cenci, chĕn′chee.
Confessio Amantis, a lover's confession.
Cophetua, cō-phĕt′ua, an imaginary African king mentioned by Shakespeare and Tennyson, besides Percy.

Dante, dăn′tē.
Deist, one who believes in the existence of God, but disbelieves revealed religion.
De Mirabili Potestate Artis et Naturæ, of the miracles of art and nature.
De Retardandis Senectutis Accidentibus, on avoiding the infirmities of old age.
De Speculis, of mirrors.
Duessa, double-minded.
Dun Edin, Edinburgh.

Epipsychidion, the little soul; a term of endearment.
Epithalamia, nuptial songs.

Fichte, fĭch′tā.
Frisia, free′zhĭ-a.

Giaour, jöûr, a dog, an infidel; a term of contempt applied by Turks to Christians.
Giotto, jŏt′tō.
Goethe or Göthe, gĕh′tā.
Guiccioli, guĭt-chē-ō′li.

Heart of Mid-Lothian, the old jail of Edinburgh, taken down in 1817.
Hengist, hĕn′gist.

Il Penseroso, the sad.

Jacobi, ya-cō′bi.

Keswick, kĕz′ĭk.

L'Allegro, the gay or merry.
Lausanne, lō-zăn′

Magna Charta, măg′ná-kär′-tá, the great charter of English liberties, signed by King John, 1215, at Runnymede.
Masaniello, mä-sá-nē-el′lō.
De Medici, dĕ mĕd′ē-chē.
Metempsychosis, transmigration of the soul.

Novum Organum, the new Instrument of Reasoning. Lord Bacon followed the title given by Aristotle — Organum — to his great work on the science of reason.

Opus Majus, the greater work (or more important writings).
Opus Minus, the lesser work.
Opus Tertium, the third work.

Perspectiva, perspective, a treatise on optics, etc.
Piers, Peter.
Pompeii, pom-pā′yee.
Principia, principles.

Salmagundi, a mixture, an olio, a medley, a miscellany.
Schiller, sçhĭl′ler.
Schleswig, sles′vik.
Schley, shly
Semitic languages are those of which Arabic is the most polished and most widely disseminated, but of which Hebrew is the most important and interesting.
Shovel-board, a game.
Sluys, slois.
Smectymnuus, the title of a work published in 1641 by five Presbyterian divines, and formed from the initials of their names, Stephen Marshall, Edmund Calamy, Thomas Young, Matthew Newcomen, William Spurstow.

Tabard, a light garment formerly worn over armor.
Tables, backgammon, so called by Chaucer, Shakespeare, Bacon, etc.
Thanatopsis, thăn′a-tŏp′sis, a view of, or meditation on death.
Toxophilus, the lover of archery.
Trialogus, a colloquy of three persons.
Turanian languages are those not Aryan or Semitic. The name is applied to the nomadic races of Asia, as opposed to the agricultural, or Aryan races.

Wieland, vē′länd.
Wycherley, wȳch′ẹr-lẹy

INDEX.

The figures in parentheses refer to the special sketches of the authors indicated.

FIRST STEPS IN GENERAL HISTORY.

A SUGGESTIVE OUTLINE.

BY ARTHUR GILMAN, M. A.

Author of "First Steps in English Literature," "Seven Historic Ages," etc., etc.

With Maps and Charts. 1 vol., 16mo, cloth, $1.12. Uniform with "First Steps in English Literature."

A. S. BARNES AND COMPANY,

NEW YORK AND CHICAGO.

THE object of this Suggestive Outline of General History is to stimulate the student to make thorough investigations, and at the same time to furnish a guide which shall indicate the general path to be pursued.

The author has presented the salient points of history with due regard to historical connection and the relative importance of the subjects treated.

Views of contemporary events are given in Tables that establish the historical connection of the nations; and Maps, that are purposely free from details, exhibit the geographic relations of the countries. The *Index* will be found of service in tracing the progress of great movements that have affected more countries than one.

"*It is not dry reading*,—chronological bones, denuded of flesh and nerve,—but general, comprehensive, yet concrete views of events grasped according to their degree of relationship."—*Professor Henry N. Day, of Yale College, in the College Courant.*

The *Hearth and Home* says: "We commend the book right heartily." "It is a thoroughly excellent one, being, in truth, the *very best of its kind* with which we are acquainted."

"Very complete. . . . . So graceful that that alone would make it popular."—*Atlantic Monthly.*

The *Liberal Christian* (New York), Rev. H. W. Bellows, D. D., editor, says: "Manuals of History are frequently far from interesting reading, and always so when made the vehicle simply of facts strung together without any vitalizing force, and burdening the mind without stimulating it.

"Mr. Gilman, however, while presenting a vast array of facts, has shown commendable discrimination in excluding all of minor interest, and *his style is admirably suited for the narration of events.* It is simple and unadorned, but *shows the thinking mind working underneath the dry narration of facts*, in the frequent reflections and bits of poetry, and the glimpses of customs and manners."

The *Massachusetts Teacher* says: "It cannot fail to be an attractive book to pupils, and a great aid to the teacher in giving the important personages and interesting events of history their chronological and geographical places."

The Rev. Edward Cooke, D. D., Principal of Wilbraham Academy (Mass.), who has used Gilman's "English Literature" with his senior classes several years, says: "The author has done a decidedly good thing. The leading points in history are treated in such a manner as to create a desire to know more. The maps are a great aid to the pupil or general reader. As a whole I regard the work a decided success."

Eben Stearns, LL. D., President of Robinson Female Seminary, Exeter, N. H., says: "'First Steps in General History' seems to me admirably adapted not only to guide a student through the mazes of history but also to assist him to keep in mind, without confusion or undue effort, the great facts which may have been the subjects of much more extensive study."

J. C. Greenough, A. M., Principal of the Rhode Island State Normal School, says: "We have long needed such a work for our schools; and I think this volume, so tastefully prepared, will have a wide sale."

Professor W. F. Allen, of the University of Wisconsin, says: "The most characteristic feature of it is *the distinctness given to the history of the several countries*. . . . . Next to this, its feature that pleases me most is the *prominence given to points which make history living and suggestive*. For so small a volume *it is surprisingly successful in this respect*."

Mrs. E. F. Hammill, Principal of the Utica Female Seminary, who has used Mr. Gilman's "Literature" several years, says of the History: "I have given it a careful and thorough examination, and find it all I expected. *The style is beautiful, clear, and concise*. It will make history delightful to young minds. I have no less than five history classes in my school."

The *Boston Christian Register* says: "It invites comparison with Mr. Freeman's 'Outlines of Universal History.' For a text-book in our common schools Mr. Gilman's book is the better adapted of the two."

The *Boston Advertiser* says: "In the arrangement, manner, and quality of its contents it could hardly be improved."

The *Boston Journal* says: "As a compact and well-arranged text-book, we know of nothing of the sort which so much as approximates this in value."

"Admirable and neatly finished." — *N. Y. Arcadian.*

"We have seen nothing better." — *Boston Congregationalist.*

"Accurate and impartial." — *Boston Literary World.*

"Full of vivacity." — *Morning Star.*

"One of the few successful attempts to popularize subjects." — *N. Y State Educational Journal.*

"He has done his work conscientiously." — *Boston Globe.*

"Mr. Gilman has the historian's sense of proportion, the journalistic talent for packing facts into small compass, and a rare facility for putting his facts and figures into readable shape." — *Chicago Advance.*

"It has many excellences." — *N. Y. Nation.*

"We cannot too highly commend this complete and trustworthy Outline of General History. . . . . It is a model of terseness and fullness combined." — *Christian Intelligencer.*

"The principles disclosed are made to appear in relation with striking and memorable events." — *Examiner and Chronicle.*

"Clearness is the chief characteristic of the volumes." — *American Educational Monthly.*

"Perhaps more correct and judicious than any other which presents so much in so small a compass." — *Standard of the Cross.*

SEVEN HISTORIC AGES; or, TALKS ABOUT KINGS, QUEENS AND BARBARIANS. 1 *vol., 16mo, with illustrations,* 88*c.*

THIS little volume will be found adapted to interest quite young children in historical reading, and is used in schools, though not expressly designed for them.

"Mr. Gilman is a scholar who knows how to write historical sketches for the young with accuracy, vivacity, and attractiveness." — *Christian Intelligencer.*

"The work is excellently done, and the book will be read by children with real pleasure." — *Literary World.*

"There is an airy grace about the little book that leaves a charming impression." — *Mrs. Horace Mann.*

"It cannot be read in families or schools, without leaving an indelible impression of the leading facts of history." — *Chicago Advance.*

www.ingramcontent.com/pod-product-compliance
Lightning Source LLC
LaVergne TN
LVHW050517100826
845148LV00002B/371